FIRST OF *ALL*

and
The
Awakenings

by

Dr. Billye Brim

First of All and The Awakenings
by Billye Brim
Paperback ISBN: 978-0-9742156-8-6

Published by
A Glorious Church Fellowship, Inc.
Billye Brim Ministries
Prayer Mountain in the Ozarks
PO Box 40
Branson, MO 65615
(417) 336-4877
www.BillyeBrim.org

Cover Design by Jared Houle
Interior Layout by Susan Lofland

Contents

PREFACE   v
1. FIRST OF ALL   1
2. PRAY IN AN AWAKENING   7
3. AWAKENINGS ON LEWIS ISLAND AND DONALD
   JOHN TRUMP   13
4. THE HAND OF GOD   21
5. JONATHAN EDWARDS AND THE GREAT
   AWAKENING   27
6. IN JONATHAN EDWARDS' OWN WORDS   33
7. THE AWAKENING OF GEORGE WHITEFIELD   45
8. AWAKENING IN OLD ENGLAND   53
9. AWAKENING IN NEW ENGLAND   63
10. GEORGE WHITEFIELD AND BENJAMIN
    FRANKLIN   69
11. GEORGE WHITEFIELD ON THE STRETCH
    FOR GOD   77
12. THE BLACK ROBED REGIMENT   87
13. COLONIAL MINISTERS AND THE DECLARATION
    OF INDEPENDENCE   97
14. PRAYER AND THE MAKING OF THE NATION   101
15. THE SECOND GREAT AWAKENING   111
16. AN AWAKENING OF PRAYER   115
17. GOD PRESERVED US A NATION   125
18. THE AUTHORITY OF THE BELIEVER   131
19. OUR MINISTRY IN THE HEAVENLIES   137
20. HOW TO MINISTER FROM THE HEAVENLIES   145
21. DO WHAT THEY DID   155
22. FIRST OF ALL FOR LEADERS   159

BIBLIOGRAPHY   163
ABOUT THE AUTHOR   167

PREFACE

One thing will save America.
And it is not the election.
It is an Awakening to God.
One thing will avail for Israel and the nations.
It is an Awakening to God.

  —Word of the Lord through Billye Brim
   June 29, 2008

CHAPTER 1

First of All

Before the 2016 election, I knew (perhaps not without a reasonable doubt) that Donald John Trump would be elected to the office of President of the United States of America.

How I knew was not through any prescience of my own, but because of supernatural revelations given to someone else. The Bible says that in the end of days believers will be given visions. The Amplified Bible calls them "divinely granted appearances." The early New Testament believers experienced them.

I was not a Trump supporter at the beginning. But I became one when in June of 2016 he and Dr. Ben Carson invited a thousand or so ministers to New York City for a "conversation." There I began to sense in my spirit that He might be God's choice.

What convinced me were visions granted to a former Muslim I will call Mike (not his real name). He had come to the Lord when He heard Jesus call him by his name—his Arabic name. Afterwards the Lord appeared to him and told him things about the Middle East. Mike's parents were what today are known as Palestinians. He grew up in Jordan.

Someone told him his visions should be judged. His pastor suggested he contact me. So Mike and his family drove ten or more hours to Branson and asked me if I would judge his visions and revelations.

First I considered what the Bible clearly states that in the end of days believers would have visions and dreams (Joel 2:28; Acts 2:16-18). And too, I was aware of the fact that Muslims were having visions and revelations of the Lord. After receiving peace in my spirit, I agreed and so began our unusual relationship.

(Just recently, I saw Author Tom Doyle on Pat Robertson's *700 Club* talking about Middle Eastern Christians undergoing great persecution, but also how they are also seeing a great harvest. He said that those who keep records of such, report that in the past ten to fifteen years more Muslims have come to the Lord than in fourteen centuries and that many have come as a result of dreams and visions. He has written a book, *DREAMS AND VISIONS: Is Jesus Awakening the Muslim World?*)

In a vision in September 2016, Mike heard the Lord say that He had prepared Donald Trump. That he would be elected. That God's purpose was to bring protection and blessing to the United States, to Israel, and to Jerusalem. It was strongly emphasized that the Body of Christ would have to pray as never before.

I knew that meant we would have to obey the Lord's command in First Timothy 2:1 as we never had.

1 Tim. 2:1 I exhort therefore, that, **first of all,** supplications, prayers, intercessions, *and* giving of thanks, be made for all men;
1 Tim. 2:2 For kings, and *for* all that are in authority; that we may lead a quiet and peaceable life in all godliness and honesty.
1 Tim. 2:3 For this *is* good and acceptable in the sight of God our Saviour;
1 Tim. 2:4 Who will have all men to be saved, and to come unto the knowledge of the truth...
1 Tim. 2:8 I will therefore **that men pray** every where, lifting up holy hands, without wrath and doubting.

THE CHURCH'S RESPONSIBILITY

Dr. Kenneth E. Hagin, whose books and publications I edited from 1970-1980, was granted a vision in which he saw three demonic frog-like creatures rise up out of the waters of the Atlantic Ocean off of Florida. They hopped along the eastern seaboard and landed in Washington D.C. He was made to know their satanic intent was to harm this nation.

He was shown, however, that this evil plan could be stopped by the prayers of the people of God. He was instructed to come back to Tulsa (he'd been on a ministry trip) and to start a regular prayer meeting to stop this strategy of the enemy. He initiated a daily prayer group, which stayed focused for a while, but let up in its initial purpose.

When the Watergate scandal with all its complexities and cover-ups caused great hurt to the nation, the Lord told Brother Hagin this was what had been revealed to him in the vision.

Then he was told something to this effect, *I'm not going to hold Richard Nixon primarily responsible for this; I'm not going to hold the Republican Party primarily responsible for this; I'm going to hold you primarily responsible for this. For I revealed it to you, and the church could have stopped it. Whatever happens in this nation happens because the church allows it to happen.*

I heard Brother Hagin say this was one of the hardest things he ever had to pray and receive forgiveness for. But he did!

FIRST OF ALL
MOBILIZATION

Considering all of this, I realize that the success of President Trump's Administration, or any future administration, falls primarily upon the shoulders of the Body of Christ.

It came into my mind, and I knew it was of the Lord, to initiate a campaign. Not a political campaign. But a spiritual campaign. A prayer campaign. A *"FIRST OF ALL" Campaign.* A campaign which calls upon believers to *commit* to pray FIRST OF ALL for our leaders just as our Lord instructs in His Word.

FIRST OF ALL before we pray for our families, before we pray for ourselves, before we pray for the lost, before we pray for our jobs or businesses, our finances, our ministries, before we pray for anything, we are instructed to pray for our leaders, for kings (today it's usually presidents, prime ministers, etc.) and those in authority.

My daughter-in-law, Candace Brim, sent me the following Andrew Murray quote: "The man who mobilizes the Christian church to pray will make the greatest contribution to world evangelization in history."

In His great plan, quite beyond my comprehension, the Lord has called and anointed me to "help the pray-ers." So through the various platforms the Lord has graciously granted me, I began to call for people to *commit.* To phone us or write us—and to say, "Count me in. I commit to pray every day FIRST OF ALL for our leaders."

If we had obeyed First Timothy 2:1 as we should have, this nation would not have known the darkness and division it has suffered. Satan (and his kingdom of darkness) is behind division. He seeks to divide and conquer.

The kingdom of the Light can and must overcome his evil plots. The most powerful weapon we have is obedience to the Word of God. And particularly concerning good government, obedience to First Timothy 2:1. We can unite in this effort and overcome the enemy's plot to destroy us through division.

COMMANDMENT WITH PROMISE

This is a commandment with promise. The revealed purpose of God is that we can expect to receive a time in which we may lead a quiet and peaceable life in all godliness and honesty. A time conducive to people being saved and coming into the knowledge of the truth.

Is this even possible in a time such as this? God didn't put a time limit on the promise. When these Holy Spirit inspired words were given through Paul, Timothy was the young pastor of the church in Ephesus. Ephesus was a wicked city that worshipped the goddess Artemis. The Roman Empire was in the throes of its most evil emperors such as Nero. Christians and Jews were thrown to lions in bloodthirsty games in the great arenas. Nero dipped them in pitch and burned them as human torches. The kings were evil. But the church was instructed to pray for them and to expect their prayers to bring about what God said they would.

If you are a believer in the truth of the Bible, you are commanded to pray first of all for your leaders, whether or not you like them. Whether or not you voted for them. Won't you please do so? And won't you please *commit* to do so? Please contact us if you would like to be counted in a huge company of praying people who are committed to pray FIRST OF ALL as our Lord commanded.

Chapter 2

Pray in An Awakening

In 1995 the Lord led me to Branson, Missouri to establish a place of prayer. It's a long story and the subject of another book, *The Road to Prayer Mountain*. Suffice it to say we now have more than 300 secluded acres that we call *Prayer Mountain in the Ozarks*.

His clear instructions were that we were to establish this place for working with Him in prayer in two ways:

1. To pray in the plans of God.
2. To stop the strategies of the enemy.

We were to provide the amenities necessary for two types of praying:

1. Individual prayers. (We have beautiful log cabins for this.)
2. Corporate prayers. (These take place in our chapel twice a week. On Sundays at 3:00 p.m. And on Wednesdays at noon central time we stream live a corporate prayer meeting that unites people in prayer from around the globe. They named themselves *The WWP's. World Wide Pray-ers.*)

INTERRUPTED

On Sunday, June 29, 2008 our 3:00 p.m. corporate prayer was interrupted. Not by a human, but by the Creator of humanity. The forty or more faithful people who regularly attended were "praying up a storm" concerning the then upcoming elections, and concerning Israel and the nations.

Suddenly something like a heavy cloak dropped on me from heaven. I've had this happen only twice since 1979. The Bible says that *"the spirits of the prophets are subject to the prophets,"* (1 Cor. 14:32). The meaning is one can speak or not speak. This is further shown in First Corinthians 14:28, *"But if there be no interpreter, let him keep silence in the church; and let him speak to himself, and to God."*

But on that Sunday afternoon, as well as the time in 1979, the words came with such power it was almost like I had to speak them or die. These words shook us. Silenced us. Even rebuked us.

> *One thing will save America.*
> *And it is not the election.*
> **It is an Awakening to God.**
> *One thing will avail for Israel and the nations.*
> **It is an Awakening to God.**

God-given thoughts then raced through my mind. I did not speak these out as I spoke the preceding utterance. I did share them with the pray-ers later. These are the thoughts that came rapid fire:

The best person in the world could be elected President and it would do no good if the people did not awaken to God. Awakenings. History. American History. The part of prayer in the Awakenings. Study.

Silenced. Shaken. We prayed about what we were to do with this. I won't go into all the details of what we were led to do, but you could sum it up like this: We were to do everything we could to pray in an Awakening. We were to pray ourselves and to influence as many believers as our God-given realm of influence provided.

DESTINY

Personally, I began to do what He said. I studied Awakenings in the history of America. The *Star Spangled Banner's* last verse calls upon us to *"Praise the Power that hath made and preserved us a nation."* I discovered how God had used Awakenings both to found and to preserve this great nation. Armed with the rich history of Awakenings in this blessed country, I taught it on television and in meetings across the United States and even in Australia and Europe.

Since then I have watched as many stirrings of Awakening have occurred. And may I say further, I believe we are on the doorstep of another great Awakening in America. In fact, I believe that Christians in America were awakened to vote in the 2016 election. I also believe that the results of that election, if supported by a church awakened to pray for our leaders as never before, can bring America to a place prepared for her by the Creator.

For He surely brought forth this nation for a destiny He

knows—and its destiny must be fulfilled for His Glory.

Once I was reading the following passage when the Lord spoke in my spirit, *I want you to notice how I had the Apostle Paul declare Me to pagans who knew nothing about Me.*

> **Acts 17:16** Now while Paul waited for them at Athens, his spirit was stirred in him, when he saw the city wholly given to idolatry...
>
> **Acts 17:22** Then Paul stood in the midst of Mars' hill, and said, Ye men of Athens, I perceive that in all things ye are too superstitious.
>
> **Acts 17:23** For as I passed by, and beheld your devotions, I found an altar with this inscription, TO THE UNKNOWN GOD. Whom therefore ye ignorantly worship, him declare I unto you.
>
> **Acts 17:24** God that made the world and all things therein, seeing that he is Lord of heaven and earth, dwelleth not in temples made with hands;...
>
> **Acts 17:26** And hath made of one blood all nations of men for to dwell on all the face of the earth, and hath determined the times before appointed, and the bounds of their habitation;

Paul declared Him as The Creator. And as The Creator who brought forth nations at particular set times and in set places. The Amplified Bible makes it even more clear.

> **Amplified**
>
> **Acts 17:24** The God Who produced *and* formed the world and all things in it, being Lord of heaven and earth, does not dwell in handmade shrines...
>
> **Acts 17:26** And He made from one [common origin, one source, one blood] all nations of men to settle on the face of the earth, having definitely determined [their] allotted periods of time and the fixed boundaries of their habitation (their settlements, lands, and abodes),

The Talmud records how God told Moses that He gave Adam

a six-day workweek with a day being a thousand years. The seventh thousand-year day will be a Sabbath.

On that time line, the United States came along late in the birth of nations. It was brought forth on the last half of the sixth day. As American History clearly reveals, it was brought forth with a destiny. To reach that destiny, we must have an Awakening to God.

CHAPTER 3

AWAKENINGS ON LEWIS ISLAND & PRESIDENT DONALD JOHN TRUMP

B efore I go into the history of Awakenings in America, I will share how I believe a long series of Awakenings in one of the remote islands of the Hebrides may have affected America's President J. Trump—though I highly doubt that he is even aware of those Awakenings. However, if I am right in my surmising about this, Lewis Island's many Awakenings may well have had an influence on the upbringing of Mary Anne MacLeod, Donald Trump's mother. And would thereby have had an effect on the upbringing of Donald Trump.

AWAKENING DEFINED

Awakenings have occurred in other nations. Northern Ireland experienced an amazing Awakening in what is known as "The Ulster Awakening (1859)." In his book *Revival Fire*, Wesley Duewel records how the Ulster Awakening coincided with "The Great Awakening of 1857-59" in America.[1] Both great moves of God, known historically as Awakenings, began with prayer. More about that later.

I introduce the Ulster Awakening here because in a book about it I found a definition that satisfied my spirit as to the difference between an Awakening and a revival. In *Ireland's Lost Heritage* I found these statements:

> A case could be made for saying that... 'a Revival' could be described as 'a visitation of God's Spirit on God's people,' but 'an Awakening' as 'a time of such intense visitation that both Christian and non-Christian communities are affected...revivals alter the lives of individuals, Awakenings alter the world view of a whole people or culture'.[2]

That's what happened in the Awakenings in America. And that's what happened in the Awakenings on Lewis Island that must have affected Donald Trump's mother. For they have affected the Island's entire population since 1820.

LEWIS ISLAND'S HISTORY OF AWAKENINGS AND REVIVALS

Much of what I quote here comes from a book, *SOUNDS FROM HEAVEN, The Revival on the Isle of Lewis, 1949-1952,* published in 2004.[3]

Although Colin and Mary Peckham's 284-page book specifically covers what is sometimes called the Duncan Campbell revival, it tells of the long series of Awakenings and their unique effects that transformed the remote island and permeated its peoples with respect for the Bible and its values.

A most important contributing factor to this uniqueness is the very geographical location of the Island itself.

The Hebrides is a series of islands forty miles west of the most northerly part of Scotland. Lewis is the most northerly island and Harris is attached to it in the south, forming one island about sixty miles long with a population of about 25,000 [in 2004]... The islands are the first to face the might of the Atlantic gales and their bleak, windswept treeless topography bears witness to the effect of the severe weather. The stretch of water between the mainland of Scotland and the Hebrides is called the Minch and currents there are such that the seafaring men of Lewis would say that it is one of the choppiest of waters to negotiate. At the time of the 1949 revival the sailings to Lewis were from Kyle of Lochalsh and Mallig to Stornoway and these journeys would take about seven hours. Seven hours on a small rolling and pitching vessel is something to be endured not enjoyed, so the Hebrides were not the popular destination of tourists and they retained their isolated position...

Lewis people are traditionally religious, with reverence for God, His Word and the ordinances of the church...

The 1949-53 revival...was conducted wholly in the Gaelic language, using the Gaelic Bible...It was hailed as 'The Lewis Revival' as if this were the only revival that Lewis had known, which of course is far from the truth.[4]

THE EARLIEST BEGINNINGS

An amazing series of outpourings of God's Spirit began with Alexander MacLeod who was born in 1786 just ten years after the American Revolutionary War.

The 1820s were to revolutionize Lewis completely... revival...swept through the whole island, including Harris...the ministry of Rev. Alexander MacLeod in Uig was enormously effective in the movement...He was to exercise a powerful and wonderfully fruitful evangelistic ministry in the island...

In his diary he records how his sermons were interrupted by the weeping of the people. The Spirit was moving in Uig and all over the island, and people were seeking God with all their hearts.

The climax came at the communion in Uig in 1828, when it was estimated that the crowd that gathered numbered 9,000. Remembering that the few roads that there were in those days were in poor condition and that the people had to cross peat bogs and rough ground on foot to get to Uig, it is utterly amazing that so many gathered in so remote a place. People walked for many miles!...

..."In 1828 the whole island seemed to be moved with one great and powerful emotion... The spirit of prayer was very marked during this time."[5]

THE LONG LASTING EFFECT OF CONTINUAL OUTPOURINGS

The outpourings of the Spirit of God on remote Lewis Island, which began so long ago and continued through so many years, must have had an effect on young Mary Anne MacLeod, Donald Trump's mother, for it seems every home on the island had a knowledge of God and a family altar.

The 1820s placed Lewis firmly in evangelical and biblical truth, gave the people to know the reality of the living God, caused them to experience the presence of God in revival, thus laying the foundation for all the many revivals that followed in many places in Lewis down the years. A new day had dawned in its history and revival was to persist in ebbs and flows from that time on...[6]

Because of its remoteness, these wonderful moves of God were not much known outside the island. They were not much publicized until Duncan Campbell came from Scotland and was recognized as the leader of the 1949-53 revival. Reverend Campbell always made the declaration that the people had prayed in the move and that it was not the first on Lewis Island.

The moves of God which began in the 1820s had good and lasting effects on the general public. The pattern was that whenever older saints who had experienced an earlier outpouring saw that the young people were drifting, they would pray in another move. The following is headed in the Peckham's excellent book as: *The Influence of Scripture and Former Revivals.* It particularly points to the conditions preceding the 1949-53 revival, but it describes how it had been since the first one.

> The young people knew the Bible, as this...was taught at school. Virtually the whole community at that stage, honoured the Word of God and respected the things of God as a consequence. They were theologically educated and many tried as much as they could to live up to that which they knew to be true, keeping the Sunday strictly as the day of worship when no work was done. This was an acknowledgement and an acceptance of spiritual things. The influences of past revivals had an enormous effect upon the lives

of the people.

Mary says, "Successive revivals in the island, since the great revival in Uig in the 1820s had brought the Scriptures into prominence in the schools and there we were taught to honour the Word of God and to memorize it. We all memorized many psalms, and whole chapters in both English and Gaelic... In our own home my unsaved father would conduct family worship each night...

This knowledge of the Word of God and the attitude to the things of God throughout the island formed a basic foundation for the Spirit to operate in unusual power. The preacher would not have to explain who Moses or Abraham or Philip or Nicodemus were. These things were known. He would not have to instruct the people in the rightness of biblical morality, for that was accepted. They knew, acknowledged and believed the Word of the Lord and accepted its standards.[7]

HIS MOTHER'S GIFT

At President Donald Trump's inauguration he took the oath of office with his hand on two Bibles. One was the Bible on which President Abraham Lincoln took his oath. The other was the Bible his mother, Mary Anne, had given him when he graduated Sunday School.

My daughter, Shelli, heard him say that his mother read them the stories of the Bible. Perhaps she carried the values of Lewis Island into her own home.

What are the odds of a young woman travelling from Lewis Island in 1930 on a hard-pitching boat seven hours just to reach the mainland of Scotland, before beginning a long trans-Atlantic Ocean voyage to America, having a son who would own a Boeing 757 jet capable of flying 500 miles per hour and who would become the President of the land she was headed toward to find a job as a household worker? Only God! I would surmise!

1. *Revival Fire,* Wesley L. Duewel, Zondervan, Grand Rapids, MI, 1995, pp. 125-160.
2. *Ireland's Lost Heritage,* David Carnduff, M.Th., IPCB Publications, printed by Antrim Printers Steeple Industrial Estate, Antrim, BT41 1 AB, 2003.
3. *SOUNDS FROM HEAVEN, The Revival on the Isle of Lewis, 1949-1952,* Colin & Mary Peckham, Christian Focus Publications, Geanies House, Fearn, Ross-shire, IV20 ITW, Scotland.
4. Ibid., p. 17
5. Ibid., pp. 28, 29
6. Ibid., p. 29
7. Ibid., pp. 83, 84

CHAPTER 4

THE HAND OF GOD

The hand of God was upon many rigorous oceanic crossings in the bringing forth of The United States of America in His timing and for His purposes (Acts 17:26). Each sailing at its God-appointed time took great faith and daring on the part of those who sailed.

DISCOVERING THE NEW WORLD

His hand was upon Christopher Columbus.

Who but God could time the sailing of Columbus' three ships on the very day the last of many shiploads of Jews was leaving from the same Spanish port. After suffering the unthinkable inhumanity of the Inquisition, Jews were exiled from Spain by royal edict in the spring of 1492. Given three months to get out, the final date by which they had to leave was the inauspicious date of the 9th of Av. *Tisha b'Av,* as it is in Hebrew, was the date both the First and Second Temples in Jerusalem were destroyed.

Columbus didn't know, nor did those forced-to-wander Jews know, that in The New World Columbus would reach, God would bring forth a nation for His purposes. One of His purposes for America was the provision of a safe haven for the Jews until He would, according to His promises, bring forth their ancient homeland in the reborn state of Israel some 456 years hence.

The journals of Columbus reveal in great detail that he believed God was leading him.

THE FIRST LANDING

God's hand had to have been upon the arduous 144-day crossing that left England December 20, 1606 and did not arrive to Virginia until April 26, 1607. Without His protection the 105 English colonists and 40 seamen could never have made what came to be known as "The First Landing."

Reverend Pat Robertson's *Christian Broadcasting Network* is located in Virginia Beach near the very spot where the colonists' first official act was corporate prayer at a place they called Cape Henry. The following is from a *CBN* article by Richard Klein:

> The settlers landed on the shores of Virginia on April 26, 1607. Before permitting the colonists to continue inland, Reverend Robert Hunt required that every person wait before God in a time of personal examination and cleansing.
>
> Three days later, on April 29, 1607, the expedition, led by Parson Hunt, went ashore to dedicate the continent to the glory of God. They carried one item with them from England for the purpose of giving glory to God in the endeavor—a rough-hewn wooden cross. As the party landed on the wind-swept shore they erected the seven-foot oak cross in the sand...

> Raising his hands to heaven, Rev. Robert Hunt
> claimed the land for country and king and consecrat-
> ed the continent to the glory of God. In covenantal
> language he declared, "...from these very shores the
> Gospel shall go forth to not only this New World, but
> the entire world."

Phyllis Mackall, who was Editor of Pat Robertson's magazine *The Flame,* was my personal friend. Her research in the
1970s had much to do with the discovery of the colonists'
prayer and cross planting and that it happened so close to
Pat Robertson's ministry. She told me how people at the
Robertson ministry were thrilled and touched by the fact
that they were a part of the fulfillment of Hunt's prayers.
CBN continues to be a spiritual force in the Hand of the Lord.
Its influence reaches from human hearts around the world
to the highest offices of The United States of America. I watch
700 Club for accurate news reporting and I pray for God's
hand to continually be upon them.

THE MAYFLOWER

That the Hand of God had to have been upon the Pilgrims'
crossing was made real to me personally when a few years
ago I walked through *The Mayflower II,* an exact replica of the
Pilgrims' ship.

I tried to imagine, and could not, the faith and courage
it took for the women, let alone the men, to board that little
ship with their families to sail across a vast ocean to parts
unknown.

After that, I read again *The Light and the Glory, God's Plan for America* by Peter Marshall and David Manuel. I learned that as they were doing research for their book, they boarded *The Mayflower II* and were as stunned as I was:

> ...we were shocked at the closeness of the quarters. One hundred and two Pilgrims had been crammed into a space about equal to that of a volleyball court. Compound that misery by the lack of light and fresh air (all hatches had to be battened down because of the stormy weather). Add to it a diet of dried peas, dried fish, and wormy biscuits, along with the stench of an ever-fouler bilge and multiply it all by sixty-six days at sea.
>
> As we emerged topside, Peter shook his head, "You know, they accepted all that with very little complaining. It was part of what they were willing to endure to follow God's will...."[1]

The Pilgrims knew they were following God's will. And so did John Winthrop who sold all his estate and sailed just ten years later.

"A CITY ON A HILL"

John Winthrop penned this oft-quoted phrase on the actual crossing of the *Arbella*. I found his exact words in their Old English spelling. And I include them here, spelled as this landed gentleman wrote them. It's not too difficult to make out their meaning. (See if you can do it.) I find the original to be so revealing of the heart of their earthly author and the heavenly hand of the Lord upon him:

Now the onely way to avoyde this shipwracke, and to provide for our posterity, is to followe the counsell of Micah, to doe justly, to love mercy, to walk humbly with our God. For this end, wee must be knitt together, in this worke, as one man. Wee must entertaine each other in brotherly affection. Wee must be willing to abridge ourselves of our superfluities, for the supply of other's necessities. Wee must uphold a familiar commerce together in all meekeness, gentlenes, patience and liberality. Wee must delight in eache other; make other's conditions our oune; rejoice together, mourne together, labour and suffer together, allwayes haueving before our eyes our commission and community in the worke, as members of the same body. Soe shall wee keepe the unitie of the spirit in the bond of peace. The Lord will be our God, and delight to dwell among us, as his oune people, and will command a blessing upon us in all our wayes. Soe that wee shall see much more of his wisdome, power, goodness and truthe, than formerly wee have been acquainted with. Wee shall finde that the God of Israell is among us, when ten of us shall be able to resist a thousand of our enemies; when hee shall make us a prayse and glory that men shall say of succeeding plantations, "the Lord make it like that of New England." For wee must consider that wee shall be as a citty upon a hill. The eies of all people are upon us. Soe that if wee shall deale falsely with our God in this worke wee have undertaken, and soe cause him to withdrawe his present help from us, wee shall be made a story and a by-word through the world. Wee shall open the mouthes of enemies to speake evill of the ways of God, and all professors for God's sake. Wee shall shame the faces of many of God's worthy servants, and cause theire prayers to be turned into curses upon us till wee be consumed out of the good land whither wee are a goeing.[2]

Winthrop referenced Jesus words, *"A city that is set on an hill cannot be hid"* (Matthew 5:14). His vision was to build a society that would be a living example of biblical values for all the world to see.

AMERICA'S HISTORY

America's history is as spiritual as it is natural. I enjoyed so much the telling of it in *THE LIGHT AND THE GLORY, God's Plan for America 1492-1793.* When the book first came out in 1977, it impacted this country. I read it then. And I have read and reread many parts of the revised and expanded edition that came out thirty-two years later.

I thrilled to the authors' descriptions of the hand of God in Columbus' dreams, in the Pilgrim's struggles, their first and second Thanksgivings, in the prayers and documents of the founding fathers with their revelations of the spiritual foundation of America.

But I leave those accounts of divine intervention and inspiration to Marshall and Manuel, as well as to other accurate sources of early American History, to focus on my subject: The Awakenings through which God—in the words of *The Star Spangled Banner's* last verse—*"made and preserved us a nation."*

---

1. *THE LIGHT AND THE GLORY, God's Plan for America 1492-1793, Revised and Expanded Edition,* Peter Marshall and David Manuel, Revell division of Baker Publishing Group, Grand Rapids, MI, p. 137.
2. 2013 The Gilder Lehrman Institute of American History, www.gilderlehrman.org

CHAPTER 5

JONATHAN EDWARDS AND THE GREAT AWAKENING

And that, knowing the time, that now it is high time to awake out of sleep: for now is our salvation nearer than when we believed" (Romans 13:11).

To require awakening an entity is either asleep or dead. That was the condition of America prior to every one of her God-given Awakenings.

How did it happen, since the New World's earliest settlers were so awake to the will of God that they gave up everything and risked their lives to follow Him?

How did it come to pass that in the 1730s the spiritual condition of the colonies had slipped so far from their beginnings?

The cause can be attributed to natural things as well as spiritual "backsliding." Widespread settlement had expanded quickly. Roads were difficult if not nonexistent. Churches were not always close at hand.

Historian Eddie L. Hyatt writes,

> By the end of the century, Winthrop's vision of New

> England being a 'shining light' and a 'city on a hill,'...
> seemed very dim indeed. Not only were many of the
> existing churches spiritually dead, but many areas,
> because of rapid population growth, were without
> churches or pastors. Sabbath breaking, profanity,
> gambling, and lewdness seemed to be everywhere.
>
> As a new century dawned, many ministers and
> laypeople alike were deeply concerned... The spiri-
> tual condition of the populace was so bleak that calls
> for special times of prayer and fasting began to be
> issued throughout the colonies by both pastors and
> government officials.[1]

Two who prayed were Reverend Jonathan Edwards and his
wife. Edwards, a descendant of Puritan pastors, described a
"general deadness throughout the land," and he and his wife,
Sarah, set themselves to pray for a "revival of religion."[2]

ACADEMIA'S ACKNOWLEDGEMENT

What happened in response to prayer affected the whole of
colonial America and birthed what even academia calls The
Great Awakening.

While I was doing what the Lord told me to do *(Study!)*
during our interrupted prayer meeting in 2008, I found that a
contemporary Harvard professor wrote that one cannot un-
derstand the colonial society that brought about the American Revolution without a study of The Great Awakening.

At the time of my study, the Longmeadow (Massachusetts) Historical Society website carried an article entitled
*The Great Awakening and Its Effect on the Society and Reli-
gion of the Connecticut River Valley,* by Meaghan McCormick.

The article stated:

> The Great Awakening was a religious movement during the 1730s and 1740s in which itinerant ministers presented powerful messages of salvation and which provided early Americans with a greater sense of nationality...one of the most notable points of origin was in the Connecticut River Valley under the leadership of Jonathan Edwards...The Great Awakening...brought about a change of values that affected politics and daily life...These attitudes were the beginnings of a sense of independence and equality that would set the stage for the American Revolution. And, as the spirit of independence was proclaimed in the colonies by the Declaration of Independence, it was often the local clergy...who rose to read to their congregations the words of that document which would spark independence in America.

When I went online to look for a definition of the word *awakening,* I was surprised that www.answers.com credited Jonathan Edwards with the word's origin.

> Word Origin: 1736
> In the winter of 1734-35, the mild-mannered Reverend Jonathan Edwards, minister of the church in Northampton, Massachusetts, was astounded. People actually were listening to his sermons and following his advice...Their talk turned to nothing but religion, and they began living godly lives. Even "the vainest and loosest!" Even young people! And this behavior was spreading from Northampton to other towns up and down the Connecticut River Valley. In a famous letter published in 1736, Edwards called this a "general awakening."

JONATHAN EDWARDS

My knowledge of Edwards before my study was limited to a somewhat vague recollection that he had preached a sermon titled "Sinners in the Hand of an Angry God."

Even one of my academic sources quelled any idea of Edwards being a hard man. At a Wake Forest University website (www.wfu.edu) I found *Lecture Four, The Great Awakening* which stated:

> ...Edwards has received a bad press for his "Sinners in the Hands of an Angry God," ...But if you read his sermons, you will find that he spoke quietly, reasonably, and logically. Indeed he was dry and even a bit boring. But he began to experience a harvest of conversions that were accompanied by exaggerated behavior. People would...shout, and run when they were converted.

Eddie L. Hyatt writes, "The response could not be attributed to Edwards' preaching style, for he was neither loud nor flamboyant in his presentation. A very logical and studious personality he wrote out all his sermons in a manuscript. He then stood behind the podium, and without moving or making any physical gestures, he would read his sermon in a monotone voice. Being nearsighted, he held the manuscript so close to his face that the congregation could not see his face."[3]

Again, I'll quote Peter Marshall and David Manuel, "Edwards had recently been preaching ever-bolder sermons against the popular notion that a person by his or her own efforts could accomplish the purposes of God, rather than solely by the enabling of God's grace...the world would be forced to take seriously Edwards' account of what was about to happen. Other theologians could not put it down to an overactive imagination; anyone who knew Edwards personally would know these phenomenal events could not have been the product of his personality...and no one was more astonished than Edwards himself. Nevertheless, he was a well-trained observer, and he did a first-class job of reporting God's lightning storm in his *Narrative of Surprising Conversions.*"[4]

1. *Pilgrims and Patriots,* Eddie L. Hyatt, Hyatt Press, PO Box 3877, Grapevine, TX. pp. 74, 75.
2. Ibid. p. 80.
3. Ibid. p. 83.
4. *The Light and The Glory 1492-1793, Revised & Expanded Edition,* Peter Marshall and David Manuel, Revell, a division of Baker Publishing Group, Grand Rapids, MI. p. 295.

CHAPTER 6

IN JONATHAN EDWARDS' OWN WORDS

In my studies, I came to feel a strong affinity toward some of the ministers of The Great Awakening. One of them was Jonathan Edwards. I came to know him best through his own writings.

What follows in the rest of this chapter is taken from a book entitled *Jonathan Edwards on Revival.*[1] In 1984, the publishers reproduced verbatim Edwards' writings first published by himself: *A Narrative of Surprising Conversions,* first published in 1736 and *Distinguishing Marks of a Work of the Spirit of God,* first published in 1741.

From here to the chapter's end you can get to know Jonathan Edwards and see The Great Awakening and how it began through his own eyes. The following is primarily from *A Narrative of Surprising Conversions.* I won't use indentation; just know this is how Edwards published it. His publication is quite lengthy, so I used ellipses to indicate omissions. The italicized words are apparently those Edwards emphasized, although I don't know in what way he did that for he, of course, wrote the account by hand.

"Section I

"A General Introductory Statement

"...The town of Northampton is of about 82 years standing, and has now about 200 families; which mostly dwell more *compactly* together than any town of such a size in these parts of the country.

"...The greater part seemed to be at that time very insensible of the things of religion, and engaged in other cares and pursuits...it seemed to be a time of extraordinary dullness in religion. *Licentiousness* for some years prevailed among the *youth* of the town; they were many of them very much addicted to *night-walking,* and frequenting the tavern and *lewd* practices, wherein some, by their example, exceedingly corrupted others. It was their manner very frequently to get together, in conventions of both sexes for mirth and jollity, which they called *frolics;* and they would often spend the greater part of the *night* in them, without regard to any *order* in the families they belonged to: and indeed *family government* did too much fail in the town. It was become very customary with many of our young people to be *indecent* in their carriage at meeting...

"There had also long prevailed in the town a spirit of contention between *two parties,* into which they had for many years been divided; by which they maintained a *jealousy* one of the other, and were prepared to *oppose* one another in all public affairs.

"But in two or three years after [Reverend] Mr. Stoddard's death [Edwards grandfather], there began to be a sensible amendment of these evils. The young people showed more of a disposition to hearken to counsel...there were more who manifested a religious concern than there used to be...

"And *then* it was, in the latter part of *December* [1734] *that the Spirit of God* began extraordinarily to set in, and *wonderfully* to work amongst us; and there were very *suddenly,* one after another, five or six persons, who were to all appearances savingly converted, and some of them wrought upon in a very remarkable manner.

"Particularly, I was surprised with the relation of a *young woman,* who had been one of the greatest company-keepers in the whole town. When she came to me, I had never heard that she was become in any wise serious, but by the conversation I then had with her, it appeared to me, that what she gave an account of, was a glorious work of God's infinite power and sovereign grace; and that God had given her a *new* heart, truly broken and sanctified...

"God made it, I suppose the *greatest occasion of awakening* to others, of any thing that ever came to pass in the town. I have had abundant opportunity to know the effect it had, by my private conversation with many. The news of it seemed to be almost like a *flash of lightning,* upon the hearts of young people, all over the town, and upon many others. Those persons amongst us, who used to be *farthest* from seriousness, and that I most feared would make an ill improvement of it, seemed to be awakened with it. Many went to talk with her, concerning what she had met with; and what appeared in her seemed to be to the satisfaction of all that did so.

"Presently upon this, a great and earnest concern about the great things of religion and the eternal world, became *universal* in all parts of the town, and among persons of all degrees, and all ages. The noise amongst the *dry bones* waxed louder and louder; all other talk but about spiritual and eternal things, was soon thrown by; all the conversation, in all companies and upon all occasions, was upon these things only, unless so much as was necessary for people carrying on their ordinary secular business. The minds of the people were wonderfully taken off from the *world,* it was treated amongst us as a thing of very little consequence...

"But although people did not ordinarily neglect their worldly business, yet *religion* was with all sorts the great concern, and the *world* was a thing only by the bye. The only thing in their view was to get the kingdom of heaven, and every one appeared pressing into it. The engagedness of their hearts in this great concern could not *be* hid, it appeared in their very *countenances*...

"There was scarcely a single person in the town, old or young left unconcerned about the great things of the eternal world. Those who were wont to be the vainest and loosest, and those who had been disposed to think and speak lightly of vital and experimental religion, were now generally subject to great awakenings. And the work of *conversion* was carried on in a most *astonishing* manner, and increased more and more; souls did as it were come by flocks to Jesus Christ.

"This work of God, as it was carried on, and the number of true saints multiplied, soon made a glorious alteration in the town: so that in the spring and summer following, *anno*

1735, the town seemed to be full of the presence of God: it never was so full of *love,* nor of *joy,* and yet so full of distress, as it was then. There were remarkable tokens of God's presence in almost every house. It was a time of joy in *families* on account of salvation being brought unto them; parents rejoicing over their children as new born, and husbands over their wives, and wives over their husbands. *The goings* of God were then *seen in his sanctuary,* God's day was a *delight,* and his *tabernacles* were *amiable.* Our public assemblies were then beautiful: the congregation was *alive* in God's service, every one earnestly intent on the public worship, every *hearer* eager to drink in the words of the *minister* as they came from his mouth; the assembly in general were, from time to time, *in tears* while the word was preached; *some* weeping with sorrow and distress, *others* with joy and love, *others* with pity and concern for the souls of their neighbours.

"Our public *praises* were then greatly enlivened; God was then served in our *psalmody,* in some measure, in the *beauty of holiness.* It has been observable, that there has been scarce any part of divine worship, wherein good men amongst us have had *grace so drawn forth,* and their hearts so *lifted up* in the ways of God, as *in* singing his praises...

"In all *companies,* on other days, on whatever *occasions* persons met together, *Christ* was to be heard of, and seen in the midst of them. Our *young people,* when they met, were wont to spend the time in talking of the *excellency* and dying *love* of JESUS CHRIST, the glory of the way of *salvation,* the wonderful, free, and sovereign grace of God, his glorious work in the *conversion* of a soul, the *truth* and certainty of the great things of God's word, the sweetness of the views of his *perfections, &c...*"

[THE AWAKENING SPREADS]

"When this work first appeared and was so extraordinarily carried on amongst *us* in the winter, *others* round about us seemed not to know what to make of it. Many scoffed at and ridiculed it; and some compared what we called conversion, to certain *distempers.* But it was very observable of many, who occasionally came amongst us from abroad with disregardful hearts, that what they saw here cured them of such a temper of mind. *Strangers* were generally surprised to find things so much beyond what they had heard, and were wont to tell others that the state of the town could not be conceived of by those who had not seen it. The notice that was taken of it by the people, who came to town on occasion of the *court* that sat here in the beginning of March, was very observable. And those who came from the neighbourhood to our public lectures were for the most part remarkably affected. Many who came to town on one occasion or other, had their consciences smitten, and awakened; and went home with wounded hearts, and with those impressions that never wore off till they had hopefully a saving issue; and those who before had serious thoughts, had their awakenings and convictions greatly increased. There were many instances of persons who came from abroad on visits, or on business, who had not been long here, before, to all appearances, they were savingly wrought upon and partook of that shower of divine blessing which God rained down here, and went home rejoicing; till at length the *same work* began evidently to appear and prevail in several other towns in the country.

"In the month of March, the people in *South-Hadley* had begun to be seized with deep concern about the things of religion; which very soon became universal... *Suffield... Sunderland... Deerfield, called Green River... Hatfield... West-Springfield... Long Meadow... Enfield... Westfield...*

"As what other towns heard of and found in this, was a great means of awakening them; so our hearing of such a swift and extraordinary propagation, and extent of this work, did doubtless for a time serve to uphold the work amongst us...

"This remarkable pouring out of the Spirit of God, which thus extended from one end to the other of this county, was not confined to it, but many places in *Connecticut... Ripton... Newhaven... Guildford... Mansfield... Tolland... Hebron... Bolton... Preston... Woodbury...*

"But this shower of divine blessing has been yet more extensive: there was no small degree of it in some part of *the Jerseys:* as I was informed when I was at New York... by some people of the Jerseys, whom I saw. Especially the Rev. William Tennent, and the minister who seemed to have such things at heart, told me of a very great awakening of many in a place called *the Mountains...* and a very considerable revival of religion in another place under the ministry of his brother the Rev. Gilbert Tennent: and also at another place under the ministry of... a Dutch minister, whose name...was Freelinghousa....

"The work in this town, and others about us, has been

extraordinary on account of the *universality* of it, affecting all sorts, sober and vicious, high and low, rich and poor, wise and unwise...*young* people, *old men*, and little *children*... A loose careless person could scarcely be found in the whole neighbourhood; and if there was *any one* that seemed to remain senseless or unconcerned, it would be spoken of as a *strange* thing....

"There are several *negroes,* who from what was seen in them then, and what is discernible in them since, appear to have been truly born again in the late remarkable season.

"God has also seemed to have gone out of his usual way, in the *quickness* of his work, and the swift progress his Spirit has made in his operations on the hearts of many. It is wonderful that persons should be so *suddenly* and yet so *greatly* changed. Many have been taken from a loose and careless way of living and seized with strong convictions of their guilt and misery, and in a very little time old things have passed away, and all things have become new with them...

"It has also been very extraordinary in the *extent* of it, and its being so swiftly propagated from town to town."

"Section II

"...These awakenings when they have first seized on persons, have had two effects; *one* was, that they have brought them immediately to quit their sinful practices; and the looser sort have been brought to forsake and dread their former vices and extravagances. When once the Spirit of God began to be so wonderfully poured out in a general way through the town, people had soon done with their old quarrels, backbitings, and intermeddling with other men's matters. The tavern was soon left empty... The *other* effect was, that it put them on earnest application to the means of salvation, reading, prayer, meditation...

"It was very wonderful to see how persons' affections were sometimes moved—when God did as it were suddenly open their eyes, and let into their minds a sense of the greatness of his grace, the fullness of Christ, and his readiness to save—after having been...under a sense of guilt which they were ready to think was beyond the mercy of God. Their joyful surprise has caused their hearts as it were to leap, so that they have been ready to break forth into laughter, tears often at the same time issuing like a flood, and intermingling a loud weeping. Sometimes they have not been able to forbear crying out with a loud voice, expressing their great admiration...

"Persons commonly at first conversion, and afterwards, have had many texts of Scripture brought to their minds, which are exceeding suitable to their circumstances, often come with great power...there is an immediate influence of the Spirit of God...

"...All things abroad, the sun, moon, and stars, the clouds and sky, the heavens and earth, appear as it were with a divine glory and sweetness upon them.

"Section III
This work further illustrated in particular instances.

"But to give a clear *idea* of the nature and manner of the operation of God's Spirit, in this wonderful effusion of it, I would give an account of two *particular instances.* The first is an *adult person,* a young woman whose name was Abigail Hutchinson...

[Eight pages in my source book cover Edwards' record of the glories Abigail experienced. I have included only a few statements herein.]

"She was of an intelligent family: there could be nothing in her education that tended to enthusiasm, but rather to the contrary extreme. It is in nowise the temper of the family to be ostentatious of experiences, and it was far from being her temper. She was, before her conversion...of a sober and inoffensive conversation; and was a still, quiet, reserved person...

"She likewise gave me such an account of the sense she once had, from day to day, of the glory of Christ, and of God, in his various attributes, that it seemed to me she dwelt for days together in a kind of *beatific vision* of God; and seemed to have, as I thought, as immediate an intercourse with him, as a child with a father...

"She often expressed a sense of the glory of God appearing in the trees, the growth of the fields, and other works of God's hands..."

NORTHAMPTON, MASSACHUSETTS
A CITY ON A HILL

News of the Awakening reached England and Dr. Isaac Watts (1674-1748), an English minister famous for his more than 750 hymns, among which is *Joy To The World.* In fact, Watts and another noted English minister, Dr. John Guyse, are listed as the first editors of *A Narrative of Surprising Conversions* by Jonathan Edwards. They wrote the preface to the first printing in 1736.

Jonathan Edwards' words at the end of that book are noteworthy, "When I first heard of the notice the Rev. Dr. Watts and Dr. Guyse took of God's mercies to us, I took occasion to inform our congregation of it in a discourse from these words—*A city that is set upon a hill cannot be hid....*"

---

1. *Jonathan Edwards on Revival,* Select Works of Jonathan Edwards, The Banner of Truth Trust, 3 Murrayfield Road, Edinburgh EH12 6EL, PO Box 621, Carlisle, Pennsylvania 17013 U.S.A. *A Narrative of Surprising Conversions.*

CHAPTER 7

THE AWAKENING OF GEORGE WHITEFIELD

When I finished (the first time I read it) John Pollock's excellent biography of George Whitefield, I literally did not want the book to end. It read with the excitement of a novel. Yet it was truth. Powerful, world-changing truth that came alive with the detailed telling of ocean crossings, hard rides through the colonial woods, rejection, yet overwhelming acceptance, as George Whitefield was (as he put it himself) "on the stretch for God." Somehow, in some small measure, it seemed I could almost feel his heart, as he lived out the answering of his amazing call to unite the American colonies into *One Nation Under God.*[1]

Without a doubt, Whitefield (pronounced Whitfield) was the leading preacher of The Great Awakening. Though many had invaluable parts, the one person to whom all historians, both secular and religious, point, as the most influential is George Whitefield.

The Restoring America Project stated, "By the time of his death in 1770, evangelist Reverend George Whitefield was the best known American in the 13 Colonies."

The Light and the Glory called him, "...the greatest evangelist of the 18th century, one of the handful of men in the history of Christendom to be used by God to change the course of nations through the power of His Spirit."[2]

HOLINESS BY WORKS

The young student, George Whitefield, was low on the social order at the class-conscious University of Oxford. John and Charles Wesley, also students, were of a higher position. Yet the three became fast friends. All yearned to "be holy" in an England where much of the populace, including the clergy, held holiness in little esteem. John led a club, formed by the Wesleys, called, The Holy Club. Its rigid rules, called "methods" by critics, eventually gained them the then derogatory name of Methodists. George joined. And there he entered a "wearisome struggle" to be holy.

> His courage failed so often. He tried to glow with the love of God when vilified, to buffet his body, regulate his waking hours, visit the poor and the prisoners, to be like the Wesleys... Twice a week George fasted. Morning and evening he meditated... when the college clock struck the hours of nine, twelve and three, he dropped whatever he was doing and recited a collect...[3]

Neither George, nor the Wesleys knew peace until they received light on, and the experience of, the new birth. George was the first to do so. And it started with a borrowed book he read, *The Life of God in the Soul of Man* by Henry Scougal, a Scot.

After reading just a little:

...George was astonished all his ideas were over-turned... he read on: "True Religion is an Union of the Soul with God, a real participation of the divine na-ture, the very image of God drawn upon the Soul, or in the Apostle's phrase, *it is Christ formed within us.*"

Whitefield blinked. He read it again—and the room seemed ablaze with light. In a second he saw, as plainly as if God had written the message in letters of fire, "I must be born again a new creature! Christ must be formed within me! I must leave no means unused which will lead me nearer to Jesus Christ."

...[He] set out in good earnest to attain the new birth. First he tried to be more humble... He resolved to give up tasty dishes... He stopped powdering his hair...

Soon he fell sick. Charles Wesley visited... as he left, [he] cracked one of the gentle jokes which made him so lovable. George laughed, but no sooner was he alone again than he decided that laughter was wrong. He must deny himself laughter if he would attain union with Christ.

When he was well again he walked with down-cast eyes and looked for happiness only in the meet-ings of the Holy Club and in church, yet felt no nearer the new birth...[4]

Six months after reading the book that started his quest for the new birth, he fasted through Lent until he was sick and weary.

The Awakening of Whitefield

The revelation of salvation solely by grace through faith struck George powerfully. So potent was its impact that it fu-eled every mile of his journey from his first breath as a new

creature in Christ to the last breath he drew before depart-
ing to glory after he'd lived an almost unimaginably difficult
and dedicated life. For this reason I include Pollock's dramatic account of George's new birth. Keep in mind as you read
it that Pollock had George Whitefield's copious and detailed
journals from which to draw so accurate an account.

Easter Day, early in April 1735, passed unnoticed.
For two or three weeks the twenty-year-old Whitefield lay almost inert eating little more than gruels
and fish... He devoted his feeble strength to praying
for the removal of his sins, and in reading his Greek
New Testament.

Another book lay unopened on his desk. He could
not remember whether he had bought it or whether
Charles Wesley—now away in the country—had left
it: *Contemplations on the New Testament* by Joseph
Hall, D.D., late Lord Bishop of Norwich. Dimly George
remembered hearing that Hall, a hundred years ago,
had withstood Archbishop William Laud only to be
evicted by Oliver Cromwell.

He opened it and at once liked Hall's tone. The
book had a calmness, an assurance which contrast-
ed with his own feverishness. Hall seemed to be en-
joying his contemplations of each phrase of the New
Testament. Every line has as it were a fatherly smile
or a compassion, which suggested a loveable, happy
author remarkably unconcerned with his own bur-
dens if, indeed, he had any.

Despite the antique language the book grew on
George... George, as he read on, reached the Crucifixion...

Now Bishop Hall addresses the Penitent Thief.
If any sinner might have sins worse than George
Whitefield's this was he, yet Hall was saying, "Thy

Saviour speaks of a present possession. *This day...*
O Saviour, what a precedent is this of thy free and
powerful grace? Where thou wilt give, what unworthiness can bar us from thy mercy?"

Still George could not get it: "*Free* and powerful
grace? What unworthiness can bar us?" He turned
another page.

Hall addresses the Saviour hanging on his Cross.
"Thou barest our sins: thy Father saw us in thee, and
would punish us in thee, thee for us."

Dimly it began to dawn for George. His mind
groped after a fact too amazing to grasp: that "*Thou
barest our sins... Thou dids't take flesh for our re-
demption.*" Man's puny efforts to redeem himself,
whether by praying in a storm in Christ Church Walk
or schooling his passions or dispensing charity, were
incapable of doing what Jesus Christ had already
done.

Had already done! Christ had already borne
the burden! The new birth was a gift, Hall showed:
"Where *thou* wilt give, what unworthiness can bar us
from thy mercy?" But to cease struggling and meekly
accept that Another had been punished in his place
was more than George could stomach. If God had
bid him do some great thing, that were easier than
to cast himself blindfold and without reserve into
God's almighty hands.

The days passed.

One afternoon the pressure on body and mind lay
unbearable as ever. George, at his desk, felt thirsty,
yet when he drank water his mouth remained dry...
He was still thirsty when his mind ranged once again
to the Crucifixion. Suddenly he recalled that Jesus on
the Cross had cried, "I thirst!"

He turned to Bishop Hall, whose words were
choice as ever: "Thou, that not long proclaimest in
the Temple, 'If any man thirst, let him come to me

and drink: he that believeth in me, out of his belly shall flow rivers of living waters,' now thyself thirstest."

It struck Whitefield that when Christ had cried out, "I thirst," his sufferings were nearly at an end.

Whitefield threw himself on the bed and called out, "I thirst! I thirst!" — his first ever cry of utter helplessness; all previous prayer had been a conscious attempt to merit God's favour.

He returned to his desk. He became aware that he was happy, as he had not been happy for nearly a year. Instinctively he knew why. He had thrown himself, at long last, blindfold and without reserve, without struggle or claim, into God's almighty hands. And Someone, unseen, but real, had slaked his thirst — had removed his burden, and replaced it with Himself.

"George!" this other seemed to say, "George, you have what you asked! You ceased to struggle, you simply believed — and you are born again!"

The sheer simplicity, almost the absurdity of being saved by such a prayer made George Whitefield laugh. At that laugh the floodgates burst.

"Joy — joy unspeakable — joy that's full of, big with glory!"

"When the Lord turned the captivity of Zion, we were like [them] that dream. Then was our mouth full of laughter and our tongue with singing."

George burst out of the room, hurried — a little unsteadily — down the staircase into God's air and the scent of blossom, and just restrained himself from slapping an astounded college porter on the back.[5]

1. *GEORGE WHITEFIELD, The Evangelist,* John C. Pollock, Christian Focus Publications, Ltd, Geanies House, Fearn, Ross-shire, IV20 1TW, Great Britain.

2. *THE LIGHT AND THE GLORY, God's Plan for America 1492-1793, Revised and Expanded Edition,* Peter Marshall and David Manuel, Revell division of Baker Publishing Group, Grand Rapids, MI, p. 298.

3. *GEORGE WHITEFIELD, The Evangelist,* John C. Pollock, Christian Focus Publications, pp. 17-18

4. Ibid. pp. 18-20.

5. Ibid. pp. 24-27.

CHAPTER 8

AWAKENING IN OLD ENGLAND

George Whitefield burst out of that room and embarked upon a journey with God that would leave in its wake Awakenings in The Old World, as well as in The New World. He crossed the Atlantic thirteen times when doing so was arduous and dangerous. A pullout map inside the cover of *George Whitefield's Journals* has on its legend: *"A Map of Mr. Whitefield's first three Voyages to AMERICA. He crossed the Atlantic 13 times and spent 732 days on the ocean travelling some 70,000 miles besides innumerable inland and coastal journeys."*[1]

George made these many crossings because, crack out of the box after his conversion, something supernatural happened when he shared or preached the wonders of salvation by grace through faith. Fires of an Awakening immediately began to burn in England.

It is said that George crossed the ocean more times than any other, except seamen. He did this to tend God's work on both sides of the Atlantic.

ENGLAND

Even before his first crossing to America, George Whitefield's ministry lit flames of fire across England. Young, slim
and good-looking, but with one "squint-eye," even George
was surprised when the anointing upon him drew never-be-
fore-seen crowds. They came to hear his sermons delivered
in a deep voice that God must have amplified, for thousands
heard him clearly across wide expanses.

Included herein are a few of the many amazing accounts, from various times, on the Old World side of Whitefield's ministry. The following is from his own journal.

> ...The sight of the congregations was awful. One
> might, as it were, walk upon the people's heads: and
> thousands went away from the largest churches for
> want of room. They were all attention, and heard like
> people hearing for eternity.
>
> I now preached generally nine times a week...
> On Sunday mornings, long before day, you might see
> streets filled with people going to church, with their
> lanthorns [sic] in their hands, and hear them con-
> versing about the things of God...
>
> The tide of popularity now began to run very
> high. In a short time, I could no longer walk on foot
> as usual, but was constrained to go in a coach, from
> place to place, to avoid the hosannas of the multi-
> tude. They grew quite extravagant in their applaus-
> es; and, had it not been for my compassionate High
> Priest, popularity would have destroyed me. I used
> to plead with Him, to take me by the hand and lead
> me unhurt through this fiery furnace. He heard my
> request, and gave me to see the vanity of all com-
> mendations but His own.

Not that all spoke well of me. No; as my popularity increased opposition increased also. At first, many of the clergy were my hearers and admirers; but some soon grew angry, and complaints were made that the churches were so crowded that there was no room for the parishoners, and that the pews were spoiled... A report was spread abroad, that the Bishop of London, upon complaint of the clergy, intended to *silence* me.[2]

The fact that George prayed extempore (rather than from authorized prayer books) and later preached extempore (rather than from a written sermon) incensed certain powers in The Church of England. Denied pulpits, he even dared, after intense soul searching, to preach out of doors.

Whitfield, and quite a bit later the Wesleys, and the crowds who came to hear, risked imprisonment under the Conventicle Act of 1664 which forbade religious assemblies of more than five people other than an immediate family, outside the auspices of the Church of England.

THE MINERS

...George had been invited to dine...with an aged Dissenter [an English Protestant who dissented with the Church of England] at Kingswood...close to the forest coal mines...where George's thoughts had often strayed...

Respectable citizens were afraid of them [the colliers]; they caused violent affrays and had shocked even the hard-bitten sailors by digging up the corpse of a murderer whose suicide had cheated them of a public execution to hold high festival round it. They were totally illiterate. Their shacks, like the mines, lay on the far boundaries of four different parishes so they were ignored by the clergy of all. Gin-devils, wife beaters, sodomites...

Their bodies might be foul but their souls were immoral. And they could only be reached in the open air. Yet to preach in the open air, John Wesley had said, was "a *mad* notion."

[From] the old Dissenter's home... George could see the forest just beyond and the trails leading to the mines. Over dinner he told their host... how "My bowels have long yearned towards the poor colliers..."

The four of them went out at the hour when many coalminers left the pits, and walked towards a rise of ground. Whitefield felt a little afraid of what he was about to do, but if the churches were to be closed against him he should all the more follow his Master's words and go into the highways and hedges. He remarked with a nervous laugh that the Lord Jesus has a mount for his pulpit and the heavens for his sounding board.

He stood on the little hill, on this Saturday, 17 February 1739, He pitched his voice about a hundred yards, to a group of colliers moving towards him. He called out: "Blessed are the poor in spirit, for they shall see the kingdom of heaven!"

The miners stopped and stared. A parson in a cassock, gown and bands, holding a book and audible at a hundred yards! That young, astonishingly clear voice came again. "Matthew, Chapter 4, verses 1 to 3." They had no idea who Matthew was... but they drew nearer, and heard... as he taught them...

By now quite a crowd had collected... George told a story which made them laugh. They had never heard a parson who cracked a joke in a sermon — but they had never heard a parson at all! ...the young clergyman's words poured out in a torrent... On and on he went, in dead silence except for his own voice and the slight stirring of wind through the bare trees behind him.

Suddenly he noticed pale streaks forming on grimy faces... Whitefield, still preaching, saw the "white gutters made by their tears down their black cheeks."

[Whitefield] received a summons to appear before the Chancellor of the diocese... Bristol shut its churches in Whitefield's face. The laity might love him. The clergy did not...

[Not long after] ...A young coalminer, his face scrubbed to a curious coffee colour found his way to... George... The miner introduced himself as Tom Maxfield... The colliers had been talking among themselves, said Tom, and they wanted Mr. Whitefield to return, not to preach to a chance crowd of passers-by but at an agreed time.

The invitation delighted Whitefield, "Blessed be God!..." he said to Seward after Tom Maxfield had returned to the mines. "I believe I never was more acceptable to my Master than when I was standing to reach those hearers in the open fields."

Little more than twenty-four hours after the Chancellor had ordered him to desist, Whitefield went back to Kingswood... Nearly two thousand people packed close around a dense mass of colliers and their families, for townsfolk too had come out on the news that Whitefield would preach in the open air. His voice came across clear: "Jesus said, Except a man be born again, he cannot see the kingdom of God!"

Highways and Hedges

After that he hesitated no longer about open-air preaching, anywhere...

The following Sunday it was known that Whitefield had been forbidden every pulpit within the city, and then a thousand Bristol folk flocked out to Kingswood to join the colliers.

"The trees and hedges were full. All was hush when I began. The sun shone bright, and God enabled me to preach for an hour with great power, and so loudly that all, I was told, could hear me. Mr. B — spoke right: 'the fire is kindled in the country. And I know all the devils in hell shall not be able to quench it.'"

Hell tried... When he preached in a big yard attached to a glassworks, a well-dressed gentleman, who was a little drunk shouted that the fellow was a dog who ought to be whipped at the cart's tail, and offered money to anybody who would pelt him with mud and stones. Some boys, however, pelted the drunk...

A climax came on Sunday, 25 March, when the weather had cleared again after a late snow. A vast congregation — estimated by the *Gentleman's Magazine* at no less than twenty-three thousand — converged that afternoon on Hannam Mount in Kingswood. Some "of the higher rank" (who once had praised his sermons in churches) came to scoff at a youth in a gown yelling from a table on unconsecrated ground. The majority however were reverent and expectant.

Whitefield climbed on the table and looked across at this unbelievable mass of people waiting for him to begin. He was struck dumb. To gain time he called out that they should sing the 100th Psalm...

Then Whitefield spoke. Standing upwind he let his voice carry right over the seas of faces, "and knew by happy experience what our Lord meant by saying, 'Out of his belly shall flow rivers of living water.' The open firmament above me, the prospect of the adjacent fields with the sight of thousands and thousands, some in coaches, some on horseback and some in the trees, and at times all affected and drenched in tears together, to which was added the solemnity of the approaching evening, was almost too much and quite overcame me."[3]

Dr. Wesley Duewel wrote in his exciting book, *Revival Fire,* "During Whitefield's time in America, revival fires...continued to burn brightly in England... Whitefield went to Scotland for the first time, and wherever he went revival flames began to burn... He interrupted this revival ministry to journey to Wales, where he married a widow of thirty-six. He himself was only twenty-six.

"At the end of 1741, he returned to Bristol and then started across England, speaking to thousands with God's power upon him. From this time on, Whitefield's routine when he was in the British Isles was to preach at his Moorfields center in London in the winter and to tour other parts of England in the summer."[4]

Wikipedia, a free online encyclopedia, has the following description of the Moorfields, which helps to explain the antics of those who railed against Whitefield in one of its sections.

> The Moorfields were one of the last pieces of open land in the City of London... The fields were divided into three areas... In the early 18th century, Moorfields was the site of sporadic open-air markets, shows, and vendors/auctions. Additionally, the homes near and within Moorfields were places of the poor, and the area had a reputation for harbour-

ing highwaymen, as well as brothels... James Dalton
and Jack Sheppard both retreated to Moorfields
when in hiding from the law.

Dr. Duewel gives a graphic account of the untoward opposition and how the anointing upon Whitefield hushed the hostile protestors, and brought a great victory.

Whitefield describes his Easter Monday at Moorfields. At 6:00 A.M. there were already about ten
thousand revelers in the spacious area. Whitefield,
with a large congregation of praying people before
him, began to preach. A hush from God came over
the worldly crowd. Many were moved to tears. At
noon Whitefield went out again. He estimates from
twenty to thirty thousand people had gathered in the
area. Opponents threw stones, dirt, rotten eggs, and
dead cats at him. But as he preached on, most of the
people became like "lambs." Whitefield announced a
third service for 6:00 in the evening.

By then, thousands more than before gathered
in the area. As Whitefield began to preach, people
deserted the entertainers and clowns in other parts
of the area. An enemy tried to strike Whitefield with
a long, heavy whip. Other opponents beat drums
to drown out his message. Despite numerous disturbances, Whitefield preached on for three hours.
Three hundred fifty people were converted that day,
and more than a thousand people handed notes to
him asking for prayer.[5]

The move of God in England was unprecedented. But always
a persistent call to the American Colonies tugged at his spirit
and took the preeminence.

Pollock wrote, "By the time he embarked for Philadelphia at last on 15 August [his second voyage in 1739] George Whitefield had preached to more people than had any man alive, probably to more than any one man before in history... But America called."[6]

1. *George Whitefield's Journals,* The Banner of Truth Trust, 3 Murrayfield Road, Edinburgh EH 12 6EL, P. O. Box 621 Carlisle, PA 17013, USA.
2. Ibid. pp. 88, 39
3. *GEORGE WHITEFIELD, The Evangelist,* John Pollock, Christian Focus Publications, Ltd., Geanies House, Fearn, Ross-shire, IV20 ITW, Great Britain. pp. 91-98.
4. *REVIVAL FIRE,* Wesley L. Duewel, Zondervan, Grand Rapids, MI. p.63.
5. Ibid. p. 64.
6. *GEORGE WHITEFIELD, The Evangelist,* John Pollock, Christian Focus Publications, Ltd., Geanies House, Fearn, Ross-shire, IV20 ITW, Great Britain. p. 120.

CHAPTER 9

AWAKENING IN NEW ENGLAND

John Pollock, Whitefield's biographer, clearly saw George's God-given vision for America. He wrote, "On his first landing in 1738 Whitefield had longed to set 'all America in a blaze for God.' ...He dared to trust that his preaching might help create one nation under God — thirteen scattered colonies united with each other, and with the Mother Country, by an Atlantic Ocean which should be a highway of exchange for gospel preachers."[1]

At the age of 23, George first arrived on American soil May 7, 1738. On the long crossing that began in January, he preached, prayed, ministered to the sick, and he himself survived sickness and its so-called *treatment.*

> Monday, May 1. This morning went out upon deck, after being confined to my bed for a week by a violent fever, with which all except three or four in the ship have been visited. I was blooded thrice, and blistered and vomited once... Satan desired to have me to sift me as wheat; but Jesus Christ prayed for me, and my faith failed not.[2]

In September he sailed back to England for two reasons set forth in the Table of Contents of his journals: "Whitefield's speedy return to England, despite his success in Georgia, is to be explained by the following reasons: (1) He wished to collect funds for the erection of an orphanage in Georgia. (2) It was necessary to return to England to be ordained a priest."[3]

NEW ENGLAND

George Whitefield set sail to return to America in August of 1739. The long, storm-wracked crossing landed in October.

He had decided to postpone his settlement in Georgia and headed to Philadelphia. He knew that for his divine call to come to fruition he had to reach New England. He would face the rigors of travelling overland through New England's colonies before heading south, also overland, to Georgia.

> Old William Tennent pricked up his ears when one of his students at the Log College told him the news: George Whitefield had ridden into Philadelphia. The City of Brotherly Love had received him with open arms; the Governor, Penn the younger, had invited him to dine and other Quakers honoured him; the Presbyterian minister and the Baptist teacher had called. The Anglican clergyman had treated him as a brother...
>
> William Tennent saddled his horse and rode off through the woods for the twenty-mile journey to the city, and rejoiced as he rode...
>
> A mutual affection sprang up spontaneously at the moment of greeting because William Tennent saw young Whitefield as the prophet he had awaited, one who should stir the embers of fires he

himself had lit long ago in his prime, while George saw in Tennent the aged standard-bearer who had been through the battle and had more to teach...

That night Tennent stood beside George as he preached from the Court House steps to a crowd which stretched away down Market Street and Second Street, as still as the stars above. Nearly every house showed lights in its upper storey. From windows open to the cool air, Philadelphians leaned out to listen.

"Father Abraham," cried Whitefield. "Whom have you in Heaven? Any Episcopalians?"

"No!"

"Any Presbyterians?"

"No!"

"Any Independents or Seceders, New Sides or Old Sides, any *Methodists?*"

"No! No! No!"

"Whom have you there, then, Father Abraham?"

"We don't know those names here! All who are here are *Christians* — believers in Christ, men who have overcome by the blood of the Lamb and the word of his testimony."

"Oh is that the case? Then God help me, God help us all, to forget having names and to become *Christians* in deed and in truth."[4]

George always saw the body of Christ as one, and mankind as equals. His view found its way into colonial hearts and pulpits.

NEW YORK

In New York Whitefield was angrily denied the use of the Episcopal Church...

"We don't want your help," said the Bishop of London's Commissary, Dr. Vesey.

Then I wish you all good luck in the name of the Lord," replied George, "I'll preach in the fields. All places are alike to me."

"Yes," sneered Vesey, "I find you are used to that."

George was disturbed nevertheless, for a mid-November evening would be no season, even for New Yorkers, to stand listening to sermons out of doors...

As if reading such thoughts the Commissary turned to George Whitefield's host, who was one of his own parishioners, and sneered again, "Mr. Noble, as you sent for this gentlemen, so I desire you will find him a pulpit." He walked out of his rectory murmuring that he had business.

Thomas Noble chose a pasture on a rise of ground in Manhattan between houses and the Hudson, and sent word round the city that Whitefield would preach at three.

A prominent New Yorker who went to hear him with considerable mental reservations found a good crowd (Whitefield was told two thousand) drawn from all denominations...and some who might never expect to enter any church.

Whitefield took his stand on a little hillock...and beckoned to the crowd to close round... He held up his hand and prayed. Whitefield began his sermon.

The New Yorker studied the twenty-four-year-old preacher: "of middle height, slender, fair and good-looking"— he was too far off for the squint! "He is of sprightly cheerful temper and acts and moves with great agility."

...This New Yorker who never had heard an extempore sermon...was amazed at Whitefield's memory. No notes, yet the discourse flowed logically and reasonably and with a delightful simplicity: no long words. Scriptures quoted copiously and explained with a marvelous faculty; "he strikes out of them such lights, and unveils those excellencies which surprise his hearers." And that voice! "He has a clear musical voice and a wonderful command of it..."

The observer turned his attention to the listeners. He noticed that though a most-attentive serious audience stood immediately round the preacher, the fringes of the crowd included some who "spent most of their time in giggling, scoffing, talking, and laughing." Whitefield soon spoke directly to these, his voice having that strange ability to sound as if he stood beside them, and they quietened. At his peroration all became hushed and still and the observer saw nothing but solemn awe and reverence as "a mighty energy attended the Word. I heard and felt something astonishing."

The anonymous New Yorker was still undecided about what to make of Whitefield and went in the evening to the Presbyterian church...

The hesitations of... his anonymous observer died that night.

"I never in my life saw so attentive an audience. Mr. Whitefield spoke as 'one having authority' all he said was Demonstration, Life and Power. The people's eyes and ears hung on his lips. They greedily devoured every word... Surely God is with this man of truth!"

And when George, for his part, looked around at this hungry audience squeezed into every niche of the church, and saw Dutch and English and a few Negroes, he cried aloud that God would destroy all bigotry and party spirit: "Some of Christ's flock are found in every denomination. My only aim is to bring men to Christ, to deliver you from false confidences, to raise you from your dead formularies, to revive primitive Christianity! If I can obtain this end, you may go to what church, and worship God in what form you like best."

...The Presbyterian minister wrote to him: "I found the next day that you had left the town under a deep and universal concern... Some who were before very loose and profligate now look back with shame on their past lives and conversations, and seem resolved upon a thorough reformation. I mention these things to strengthen you in the blessed cause you are engaged in, and support you under your abundant labours."[5]

1.   GEORGE WHITEFIELD, The Evangelist, John Pollock, Christian Focus Publications, Ltd., Geanies House, Fearn, Ross-shire, IV20 ITW, Great Britain. pp. 227 and 122.
2.   George Whitefield's Journals, The Banner of Truth Trust, P. O. Box 621, Carlisle, PA 10713.
3.   Ibid. p. 23.
4.   Ibid. pp. 123-125.
5.   Ibid. pp. 125-127.

CHAPTER 10

GEORGE WHITEFIELD AND BENJAMIN FRANKLIN

In all thy ways acknowledge him, and he shall direct thy paths (Proverbs 3:6).

Recently I looked back at my life and took a somewhat chronological mental account of how God directed me to meet and know others for His divine purposes. I told my son, Chip, about it and how it was almost like connecting the dots to see how I got where I am. Chip said, "Those are God dots."

Surely God directed the crossing of the paths of George Whitefield and Benjamin Franklin. It was for God's purpose in bringing forth The United States of America.

In 2015 Eddie L. Hyatt asked me to write an endorsement for a book he had written. This is what I wrote. It was included in the front matter of *The Faith & Vision of Benjamin Franklin:*[1]

> As always, Eddie Hyatt brings us a well-researched history book that reads as pleasurably as a novel. Benjamin Franklin has been so used and abused by revisionists who want us to doubt the spiritual beginnings of the United States of America. I have so enjoyed this account of Franklin's faith, which is something of a restoration of this founding father's

reputation as a believer. George Whitefield is my friend by means of studying his part in The Great Awakening out of which this country was birthed. How wonderful to know, via Hyatt's book, that he was also a longtime friend of Benjamin Franklin.

Hyatt recorded in detail, the Providential meeting and subsequent friendship of these two great men. He wrote, "He [Whitefield] arrived in Philadelphia in the fall of 1739, and his preaching had an immediate and profound impact on the city. No building in Philadelphia was large enough to accommodate the thousands who flocked to hear him preach, and he was forced to preach outdoors. The meetings were nonsectarian, and in his *Autobiography* Franklin wrote,[2]

> In 1739 there arrived among us from Ireland the Reverend Mr. Whitefield who made himself remarkable there as an itinerant preacher. He was at first permitted to preach in some of our churches, but the clergy, taking a dislike to him, soon refused him their pulpits, and he was obliged to preach in the fields. The multitude of all sects and denominations that attended his sermons were enormous, and it was a matter of speculation to me, who was one of the number, to observe the extraordinary influence of his oratory on his hearers. It was wonderful to see the change soon made in the manners of our inhabitants. From being thoughtless or indifferent about religion, it seemed as if all the world were growing religious so that one could not walk through the town in an evening without hearing psalms sung in different families of every street.[3]

Under the heading *Whitefield Fans the Flame of the 'Great Awakening,'* Hyatt wrote, "Although accounts of his meetings often describe the multitudes as standing and listening in rapt silence, accounts also reveal intense emotional responses experienced at times to his preaching, as well as spiritual manifestations, such as weeping, falling, and crying aloud to God. On one occasion, after preaching to a huge throng gathered outdoors, Whitefield surveyed the crowd and noted the amazing response,

> Look where I would, most were drowned in tears. Some were struck pale as death, others wringing their hands, others lying on the ground, others sinking into the arms of their friends and most lifting up their eyes to heaven and crying out to God.

"The 'Great Awakening,' as it came to be known, spread up and down the eastern seaboard, thanks in great part to Whitefield's untiring labors and nonstop travels. Everywhere he went, huge crowds turned out to hear him preach. In Boston, a massive crowd, that some estimated at 25,000 — more than the population of the city — gathered on Boston Common to hear him preach. He became the most recognizable figure in Colonial America, as a result.

"In his *Autobiography,* Franklin admits that he was skeptical of reports of Whitefield's preaching being heard by crowds of 25,000 and more. So, with his enquiring, scientific mind, he devised a way to settle it for himself. On one occasion, while Whitefield was preaching to a huge crowd from the top of the Philadelphia Courthouse steps, Franklin stepped off the distance to which Whitefield's voice could be heard:[4]

> Imagining then a semi-circle of which my distance would be the radius, and that it was filled with auditors, to each of whom I allowed two square feet, I computed that he might well be heard by more than thirty thousand. This reconciled me to the newspaper reports of his having preached to twenty-five thousand people in the fields.[5]

FRANKLIN'S FRIENDSHIP WITH WHITEFIELD

I took the liberty of borrowing Hyatt's heading for what he wrote under it:

> Whitefield visited Philadelphia many times. On his first visit, he was introduced to Franklin who was eight years his senior. This proved to be the beginning of a close friendship that lasted until Whitefield's death 31 years later. Franklin...devised an arrangement to print and distribute Whitefield's sermons and journals. It was a win-win deal, providing increased business and income for Franklin, while allowing Whitefield to expand his influence through the printed page.[6]

I read the following anecdote in several accounts of Whitefield's life. Hyatt's telling of it, however, included the revealing information that it came about after Whitefield rejected Franklin's advice on relocating his orphanage.

Whitefield sought Franklin's advice in business matters related to his ministry, not only concerning the printing and distribution of his sermons, but also concerning the establishment of an orphanage in Georgia. In this regard, Franklin tells a humorous, personal story to illustrate the power of Whitefield's preaching.

Franklin had advised Whitefield to bring the orphans to Philadelphia and to build the orphanage there instead of putting out the extra expense involved in shipping building materials to Georgia. Whitefield rejected this advice, and so Franklin decided he would not contribute to the project.

Not long after this decision, Franklin was attending one of Whitefield's outdoor meetings. Toward the end of the sermon, he perceived that Whitefield was about to receive an offering for the orphanage. He said, "I silently resolved he should get nothing from me."

His resolve, however, wilted under Whitefield's preaching and he wrote,

> I had in my pocket a handful of copper money, three or four silver dollars, and five pistoles in gold. As he proceeded I began to soften, and concluded to give the copper. Another stroke of his oratory made me ashamed of that, and determined me to give the silver; and he finished so admirably that I emptied my pocket wholly into the collector's dish, gold and all.

...Whitefield made seven visits to America and always spent time with his printer friend in Philadelphia. Before one of these visits, he wrote Franklin a letter informing him that his normal place of lodging in Philadelphia was not available... Franklin heartily welcomed him to stay in his home, and the evidence indicates that Franklin's home became Whitefield's home when he was in Philadelphia.

...They continued to correspond.... Franklin once said to his brother James, "Whitefield is a good man and I love him."[7]

THE VISION
UNITY UNDER GOD

You will not find the details of the following proposal in most books pushing the idea that Franklin, born of Puritan heritage, leaned to Deism throughout his life. But Eddie Hyatt records a revealing proposition:

In 1756 Franklin proposed that he and Whitefield partner to establish a new colony in Ohio that would honor God and advance the Christian faith. He wrote,

I imagine we could do it effectually and without putting the nation at too much expense. What a glorious thing it would be, to settle in that fine country a large strong body of religious and industrious people! What a security to the other colonies; and advantage to Britain, by increasing her people, territory, strength and commerce. Might it not greatly facilitate the introduction of pure religion among the heathen, if we could, by such a colony, show them a better sample of Christians than they commonly see in our Indian traders....[8]

Comparing his life to a drama and himself in the "final act," Franklin explained that he would like to "finish handsomely" by giving himself to such a project. "In such an enterprise," he said, "I could finish my life with pleasure, and I firmly believe God would bless us with success."

...Due to time, distance, and various circumstances, the specific venture was not executed. But, I would suggest that Franklin's vision of a Christian colony did not die, but, in fact was fulfilled on a much larger scale, beyond what he could have imagined. It was twenty years after the date of the original proposal that Franklin, along with 55 others, signed the Declaration of Independence, bringing into existence a new nation — one built on Christian values of faith and freedom.[9]

LIFETIME FRIENDSHIP

When Whitefield died in 1770 these two giants in American History had walked together a long time. Franklin was in London at the time of his good friend's passing. When he received word, he wrote:

I knew him intimately upwards of thirty years; his integrity, disinterestedness, and indefatigable zeal in prosecuting every good work, I have never seen equaled, I shall never see exceeded.[10]

Whitefield's "indefatigable zeal" was perhaps the most powerful force energizing, under the hand of God, The Great Awakening.

1. *The Faith & Vision of Benjamin Franklin*, Eddie L. Hyatt, Hyatt Press, P. O. Box 3877, Grapevine, TX 76099.
2. Ibid. p. 32
3. *The Autobiography of Benjamin Franklin*, Benjamin Franklin, New York: Airmont, 1965, p. 14.

4. *The Faith & Vision of Benjamin Franklin,* Hyatt, p. 35.

5. *The Autobiography of Benjamin Franklin,* Franklin, p. 103.

6. *The Faith & Vision of Benjamin Franklin,* Hyatt, pp. 35, 36.

7. Ibid. pp. 37, 38

8. *George Whitefield: America's Spiritual Founding Father,* Thomas S. Kidd, New Haven: Yale University Press, 2014, p. 211.

9. *The Faith & Vision of Benjamin Franklin,* Hyatt, pp. 40-42.

10. *George Whitefield: America's Spiritual Founding Father,* Kidd. p. 253.

CHAPTER 11

GEORGE WHITEFIELD ON THE STRETCH FOR GOD

I practice and I preach a valuable lesson I learned from Jeanne Wilkerson, a highly esteemed woman of God. Mrs. Wilkerson walked in an intimacy with the Lord that very few know. She experienced it through many years of prayer.

Being in a service where she ministered, one knew that what she spoke came from an intimate fellowship with her Lord. Though she has been in Heaven since 1987, one can still experience a taste of it through her book, *Contact With God: The Amazing Power of Prayer,* or in videos we have of her teaching at Rhema Bible College in Tulsa.

For many years, Jeanne taught at a church in Tulsa to an always packed out Sunday School class. But she did not travel in ministry. She prayed. She and her small prayer group prayed every night, taking no vacations, during the Vietnam war.

Later in her life, the Lord led her to go out in ministry and to share what she'd learned at His feet. Wherever she went, her hosts had usually never been so close to one who carried such a presence of God. Quite often this led to an unintended abuse of the gift she carried.

For instance, she would minister at a church on Sunday morning. Then the pastors would invite others and take her to lunch where they urged her to keep on sharing. Afterwards she would preach on Sunday night. And perhaps she would start a week of meetings the next day. This wore on her body.

One day, in the pulpit, she swooned and fell. They rushed her to the hospital where the diagnosis was extreme fatigue. Several days of hospital rest were ordered.

After a few days of rest, she said the Lord spoke to her.

"Do you know how long the Babylonian captivity was?" He asked.

She knew. She was an outstanding Bible scholar and teacher. So she answered the One she knew so well, "Yes, seventy years."

"Do you know what determined the length of that captivity?"

"Yes. It was determined by the number of years Israel did not let the land rest." (According to Leviticus 25, Israel was to let the land rest unsown every seventh year.)

"That's right, they didn't let the land rest so it took a forced rest," the Lord said. And then He asked, "Now what is it your body is made of?"

"Dirt." She got the message.

"It is written that I made the Sabbath for man, not man for the Sabbath. When you do not take a Sabbath's rest your body, made of the dust of the earth, will take a forced rest. That's what happened to you."

My being mentored by Jeanne Wilkerson was one of those "God dots" in my life. So remembering this lesson, and something else I heard from a wise man of God, I do rest.

What that man of God said was in response to what someone had said to him:

"I'd rather wear out than rust out."

(They probably had no idea that was a phrase George Whitefield used when people urged him to rest.)

The minister's sound response was, "You don't have to do either, wear out or rust out, if you pace yourself."

So I pace myself and I'm active and healthy. And, like I said, I both practice and preach it.

However, there are exceptions to every rule. And I have come to believe that it was necessary in the plans and purposes of God that Whitefield went at an unimaginable pace "on the stretch for God."

A LIFE ON THE ALTAR

His own journals and Pollock's biography record in detail the pace George Whitefield kept — and the resulting stress on his life totally dedicated to what he believed was his call to America. Space does not allow the detailed accounts given of his thirteen ocean crossings, his miles and miles of traveling by horseback, his almost never refusing a request for preaching, his work with the orphans, the slaves, the native Americans, and his bouts with sickness, many of which he preached right through them.

> Everywhere he went, revival accompanied him...
> Even when he came unexpectedly to a town, there
> was an astonishing turnout. For example, there was
> the time he felt that God wanted him to change his

itinerary at the last minute and preach at Middletown, Connecticut. The moment they knew he was coming, riders galloped down all the roads ahead of him, spreading the word that the man who had preached in Philadelphia "like one of the old apostles" would soon be preaching in front of the meetinghouse. Farmers dropped their hoes, left their plows, grabbed their wives, and mounted their horses. One observer described a sound like distant thunder, and he saw a great cloud rising along the road — everyone was riding as fast as possible down the dirt roads to Middletown. When Whitefield arrived, several thousand horses had been tethered in long lines at the back of a vast crowd of dust-covered farmers. It looked as if an entire cavalry division had dismounted and was awaiting him.[1]

Peter Marshall and David Manuel in their book, *The Light and The Glory,* really capture the fact that his "indefatigable zeal" was probably a necessity for the new nation that would be born very soon after his death.

And so it went, year after year, up and down the East Coast and as far inland by canoe and horseback as civilization extended. For Whitefield loved the frontier; and next to actually preaching, he was happiest in the saddle, seeing new terrain and meeting new people. In the summer of 1754 he wrote Wesley,[2]

My wonted vomitings have left me, and though I ride whole nights and have frequently been exposed to great thunders, violent lightnings, and heavy rains, yet I am rather better than usual, and as far as I can judge am not yet to die. O that I might at length begin to live! I am ashamed of my sloth

and lukewarmness, and long to be on the stretch
for God.[3]

It is a true mark of his spirit that George Whitefield
should be ashamed of his sloth in the same year in
which he preached a hundred times in six weeks, riding the main roads and throughout the backwoods
of New England, covering nearly two thousand miles
in five months.

He drove himself unmercifully, and it did exact a
fearful toll on his health. But no matter how sick he
was, as long as he had the strength to stand and the
breath to speak, he would preach and would trust
God to sustain him through the sermon and to provide the power and the anointing.

The Lord never failed him.

...Had he driven himself any less hard, had he
gone easy on himself, would the tremendous work
that God purposed through him have been accomplished?

For the Lord, through the preaching of this cov-
enanted man, was uniting the thirteen colonies —
on a level so deep that few people even realized
first what was happening. But wherever Whitefield
went, he was preaching the same Gospel. The same
Holy Spirit was quickening his message on people's
hearts, and Presbyterians, Congregationalists, Baptists, Episcopalians, Catholics, Quakers, Moravians
— all were receiving the same Christ in the same
way. In so doing, as Pollock points out, Whitefield
"was the first man to cut across denominational
barriers..."

In Charleston people were discovering that Jesus
died for their sins, that He could and would forgive
sin, and that they need not continue any longer under the bondage of sin. In New Haven, Providence,
Peekskill and Baltimore, they were making the ex-

act same joyous discovery. And because this was so important — more important than anything else in their lives — geographical barriers became no more significant than denominational ones. They were still there, but they were inconsequential alongside the magnitude of their shared experience.

They were beginning to discover a basic truth that would be a major foundation stone of God's new nation, which by 1776 would be declared self-evident: that in the eyes of their Creator, all people were of equal value. By the sovereign acts of Almighty God, and through the obedience of a few dedicated people, the Body of Christ was forming in America.

Through the universal, simultaneous experience of the Great Awakening, Americans began to become aware of themselves as a nation....[4]

THE SUN SETS AND ARISES

As I wrote earlier, when I studied American history and the Awakenings as the Lord told me in June 2008, I met and, like Franklin, loved the man George Whitefield.

Twice I have taught on Awakenings on *The Believer's Voice of Victory* television program and, of course, on George Whitefield as the leading figure of The Great Awakening. The first time, when we came to the end of his earth life, I read the account of his passing. A Presence came upon the set. Gloria Copeland and I wept. Quietly. The camera operators and all the crew wept. Quietly. It was almost as if Whitefield's life in the service of the Lord and for America was being honored from the Unseen Realm.

Much of the account I read that day was from *The Light and The Glory.* David Manuel, one of its authors, was my personal friend. I was one of several who gave the Eulogy at David's Homegoing service in April 2013. I think he and Peter Marshall, whom I also met by telephone, would be honored to be a part of the book you are reading now. So in their words:

> We wondered, as we came to the closing pages of Whitefield's story, if part of the tremendous urgency he felt at the end of his life was Spirit-given — if indeed God was requiring of him a superhuman effort to spread the Light as far and as quickly as possible. In 1770, his health now broken and his breathing tormented by asthma attacks, he drove himself as never before. He reached Boston on his last visit, on August 15, five months after British troops had fired into a mob of civilians, killing five and igniting a fury of protest. That incident, known thereafter as the Boston Massacre, had helped to create a hunger in the city for Whitefield's preaching. Never had the crowds been larger, nor "the word received with greater eagerness than now. All opposition seems as it were, for a while to cease."
>
> The next month found him up in New Hampshire, where the ministers of Exeter begged him for a sermon. But when the time came, he could barely breathe, and one of them said to him, "Sir, you are more fit to go to bed, than to preach."
>
> "True, sir," gasped Whitefield. Then, glancing heavenward he added, "Lord Jesus, I am weary in Thy work, but not of it. If I have not finished my course, let me go and speak for Thee once more in the fields, and seal Thy truth, and come home and die!"[6]

Pollock wrote, "Whitefield stood up on the hurriedly erected platform as if exhausted by thirty-three years of preaching, his face bloated, his breath heavy. In a low voice he announced a text: 'Examine yourselves whether ye be in the faith.' He stood silent. Minutes passed. He said, 'I will wait for the gracious assistance of God. For he will, I am certain assist me once more to speak in his name.' Then he began. The words came hoarse and sluggish at first, the sentences disjointed and rough as if his brain refused to focus. He spoke of men's attempt to win the favour of God by good works and not by faith. George contemplated, as if thinking out loud, the enormity of such effrontery. His mind suddenly kindled and his voice rose and he thundered in tones that reached the edge of the immense crowd: 'Works? Works? A man get to heaven by *works?* I would as soon think of climbing to the moon on a rope of sand!'

"After that any weakness seemed engulfed in a mighty power that swept him into an unforgettable sermon in which he proclaimed, once again, the Glories of Christ...."[7]

Then, according to Jonathan Parsons, the minister of Newburyport, he seemed to be rekindled by an inner fire. His voice now strong and clear, he preached for an hour with such tremendous power that Parsons could write, "He had such a sense of the incomparable excellencies of Christ that he could never say enough of Him." On and on he went, into the second hour, and seeming to look right into heaven, "he felt the pleasures of heaven in his raptured soul, which made his countenance shine like the unclouded sun." Nearly two hours had passed when he cried out: "I go! I go to rest prepared. My sun has arisen and by the aid of Heaven has given light to many. It is now about to set... No! It is about to rise to the zenith of immortal glory... O thought divine! I shall soon be in a world where time, age, pain and sorrow are unknown. My body fails, my spirit expands. How willingly I would ever live to preach Christ! But I die to be *with* Him!"

That night he was put to bed in the parson's home and had a fitful sleep. In the early morning, despite a crushing pain in his chest, he nonetheless pulled himself out of bed and made his way over to the window to see the dawn's early light. George Whitefield died just as the first rays of the sun caught the waters of the bay below.

The new day would soon break across the nation. His dream had come true: America was a nation now — one nation under God.[8]

Unto a Good Land, A History of the American People, by David Edwin Harrell, Jr. and a team of historians concludes, "To be sure, Whitefield did not do it alone, though it is worth noting that the first individual to bring some degree of unity to the colonies was not a politician but a preacher."[9]

---

1. *The Light and The Glory,* Marshall and Manuel, Revell division of Baker Publishing, Grand Rapids, MI. p. 303.
2. Ibid. p. 304.
3. *George Whitefield, The Evangelist,* John Pollock, Christian Focus Publications, Ltd. p. 246.
4. *The Light and The Glory,* Marshall and Manuel, pp. 305-306.
5. *George Whitefield, The Evangelist,* Pollock, (This quote and the following quotes, pp. 268-270.)
6. *The Light and The Glory,* Marshall and Manuel, p. 307.
7. Ibid. p. 268.

8. *The Light and The Glory,* Marshall and Manuel, p. 308.
9. *Unto a Good Land: A History of the American People,* David Edwin Harrell Jr. Edwin S. Gaustad, John B. Boles, Sally Foreman Griffith. ISBN-13: 978-0802837189.

CHAPTER 12

THE BLACK ROBED REGIMENT

When the brochure for *"The Next Great Awakening Tour, June and July 2010"* came across my desk, Oh! How I wanted to take it. But I didn't see how I could. I'd push it aside. But it always found its way back to the top with its inviting lead: *An Historical Tour of Boston, New York, Philadelphia, Washington, D.C., including Harvard, Yale & Princeton... Tour the sites of previous awakenings as we anticipate the next one.* It would be led by David Barton, American history expert who emphasizes its biblical roots, and Dr. Jim Garlow, pastor and political activist! It would feature guest appearances by outstanding leaders, spiritual, political, and academic. When I finally called about it, I got the last seat available on this one-bus tour.

I can't begin to tell you how this once-in-a-lifetime tour both enhanced and taught me so much more about what I had been studying at the Lord's direction.

One memorable moment was when I stood on the Lexington Common, where the first shot of the Revolutionary War was fired. I was struck by the fact that the Colonial militia involved was made up mostly of men from Reverend Jonas

Clarke's congregation. I became personally impacted by the place of the clergy and "The Black Robed Regiment" in The American Revolution. It became so real to me that America did in fact know its civil beginning from its spiritual Awakening.

Harvard professor, William Perry, said, "The Declaration of Independence of 1776 was a direct result of the evangelical preaching of the evangelists of the Great Awakening."[1]

CULTURAL CHANGE

Like the definition of an awakening and how it differs from a revival, which I quoted earlier, The Great Awakening brought about cultural change.

> The Great Awakening literally changed the moral climate of colonial America. Entire communities were transformed. Profanity, lewdness, and drunkenness almost completely disappeared, especially in some areas. Reports in New England alone show thirty thousand to forty thousand converts and 150 new churches.[2]

> The Great Awakening also greatly advanced the cause of education in America. Princeton University was born out of the work of William Tennent Sr. and his Log College. Several other early centers of education, such as Rutgers University, the University of Pennsylvania, and Brown University, had their beginnings in the wave of enthusiasm from the Awakening.[3]

And, of course, The Great Awakening affected the pulpits of most colonial churches. The preachers' belief in a united nation under God and in its right to freedom found its way into their sermons and into colonial hearts and souls.

TYRANNY

The tyrannical acts of King George III toward the American colonists, proved more and more intolerable. In fact a series of laws he issued to quell colonial resistance came to be known as "The Intolerable Acts."

Colonists were angered by unfair "taxation without representation." The Stamp Act. The Townshend Act. The sending of British governors and tax regulators to oversee burdensome tariffs. The increased size of the British garrison in America. Etcetera. Etcetera. Etcetera.

Acts of rebellion followed. What became known as The Boston Massacre in 1770. The Boston Tea Party in 1773 led by Samuel Adams and the Sons of Liberty. The forming of militias. The stockpiling of arms.

> As usual, American opinion on this mounting crisis was largely shaped by the ministers. These men of God who were American-born and not in Crown colonies (such as Georgia and Virginia) were becoming nearly unanimous in their support of resistance. Thanks to the Great Awakening, there was now a whole new generation of committed clergy salted throughout America, many of them ministers of considerable spiritual depth and maturity.
>
> As the list of "intolerable acts" mounted, so did the remonstrations against them — almost as if the ministers had George III in the front row of their congregations and were trying to make him see the

error of his ways. Many of their sermons were duly printed in town newspapers...[4]

THE SHOT HEARD AROUND THE WORLD

Our tour group stood on the now park-like area of the Lexington Common where the colonial militia met the invading British troops in the first battle of The War of Independence. A New England pastor and historian dressed as an American Colonial gave us a dramatic account of that fateful day, April 18, 1775. He pointed to the site of Pastor Jonas Clarke's church just a few yards away and down the street a block or so to the Clarke home.

> ...Since the struggle over the Stamp Act in 1765, this clergyman had become this town's principle leader in its town meetings and issues of liberty and government... His home was a frequent meeting place for men like Samuel Adams and John Hancock when safe locations could not be assured inside Boston. Such was the case on the night of April 18, 1775. Adams and Hancock were visiting for the night, unaware that the British had decided to send troops to Lexington to destroy the town's military supplies and capture these two men. One of Clark's house guests asked him on that night if the Lexington people would fight if necessary. Clark, who had laid a solid foundation concerning the duty of self-defense of inalienable rights for years through his sermons, responded confidently: "I have trained them for this very hour!"[5]

This was the night of the famous ride by Paul Revere. Orders were given to hang lanterns in the North Church Steeple according to the agreed upon signal "one if by land, two if by sea." Revere saddled up and rode toward Lexington to declare the Red Coats are coming.

> After several adventures on the way, in which he narrowly escaped capture, he reached the house of Mr. Clark about midnight... Revere found the family at rest, and a guard of eight men stationed at the house, for the protection of Adams and Hancock. He rode up, and requested admittance, but the Sergeant replied that the family before retiring had desired that they not be disturbed by any noise about the house. "Noise! You'll have noise enough before long. The Regulars are coming..."[6]

About one o'clock on the morning of the 19th, seventy odd members of the militia, largely made up of Clark's congregation, formed a line on the Lexington green near the meeting house. It was commanded by a deacon, Captain John Parker. "Stand your ground!" he called out. "Don't fire unless fired upon. But if they want to have a war, let it begin here!"

And indeed, it did begin. For someone (evidence points to a British soldier) fired the famous "shot heard round the world."

But the battle on the green, as the British Regulars fired upon the colonials was called by one historian, "a field of murder not of battle." Nine minutemen were killed and ten wounded.

The British were masters of the field in Lexington. Buoyed by success they marched on to Concord. But from here on they met with different circumstances.

"The Battle of Lexington had lasted less than a quarter of an hour. But for the British, a long day — the first of an eight-year ordeal — was just beginning."[7]

Captain Parker, seeing the approach of seven hundred British Regulars marching toward them, and realizing how badly outnumbered they were, had ordered his men to disperse from the common. They faded out of the area and rode through the countryside gathering men as they went. "To arms, to arms! The war's begun. They're heading to Concord," a rider would cry. Farmers for miles around left their fields, picked up their muskets, and headed to their militia assembly points.

Less than an hour after the British fired on Lexington militia, word reached Concord, where the town's militia was already mustered. William Emerson, Concord's minister turned out on the common in his black robe to stand with the militia. While the men nervously awaited the arrival of the British troops, the townspeople hastily hid the stores of the armory in basements, fields, and attics. Emerson noticed that one of his flock, an eighteen-year-old named Harry Gould was trembling. In clear tones, he reassured him: "Stand your ground, Harry! Your cause is just, and God will bless you." Thus encouraged, Gould went on to distinguish himself in the actions of the day.

...The British soldiers were shocked. These farmers had not scurried away at the first volley, as those at Lexington had seemed to. Here they stood their ground and calmly returned fire. And they could shoot.[8]

Pitcairn burned the ammunition depot and ordered a withdrawal and began a retreat to Boston.

> The Americans, however, fired on the retreating British, who fired back. The patriots had learned to fight in the manner of the local natives, and knowing the terrain, they were able to take shortcuts and ambush the retreating British from behind trees, stone walls, barns, and from wherever they could find cover.
>
> The patriots harassed the British all the way back to Boston. At times, the British soldiers panicked, with some throwing away their weapons as they sought to outrun the patriots...
>
> No King But Jesus
> Before the first shot was fired in Lexington, Rev. Clarke made a strategic declaration. It was a spontaneous response to Major Pitcairn's demand to the Minutemen, "Disperse, ye villains, lay down your arms in the name of George the Sovereign King of England." Rev. Clarke shouted, "We recognize no Sovereign but God and no king but Jesus."
>
> That cry caught the imagination of American patriots everywhere, and soon it was heard throughout the colonies.[9]

THE BLACK ROBED BRIGADE

It was the British who labeled the Colonial preachers the Black Robed Brigade. And they attributed the Revolutionary War and its American victory to the ministers who wore black robes in their pulpits. Not only did they preach, however, they practiced what they preached.

Significantly, many who awaited them along the road [from Concord back to Boston] were local pastors, such as the Rev. Phillips Payson and the Rev. Benjamin Balch, who had heard of the attack, taken up their own arms, and then rallied their congregations to fight the returning British. But pastors from other areas also responded. When word reached Vermont, the Rev. David Avery promptly gathered twenty men and marched toward Boston, recruiting additional troops along the way, and the Rev. Stephen Farrar of New Hampshire led ninety-seven of his parishioners to the scene of danger.

A few weeks later at the Battle of Bunker Hill, American ministers again delved headlong into the fray. When the Rev. David Grosvenor heard that the battle had commenced, he left from his pulpit, rifle in hand, and promptly marched to the scene of action, as did the Rev. Jonathan French; and the Rev. Joseph Willard raised two full companies and led them to the battle.

This pattern was common through the Revolution... Of Rev. John Craighead it is said that "he fought and preached alternately." ...And there are many additional examples...[10]

THEY TOOK YOUR VOICE AWAY

During the 2016 Presidential Campaign, I was invited along with a thousand ministers to New York City for a "Conversation with Donald Trump and Ben Carson."

Alluding to the Johnson Amendment (a provision in the tax code that prohibited non-profit organizations from endorsing or opposing political candidates), then candidate

Trump said to the ministers, "Don't you know they took your voice away?"

I wonder if the Black Robed Brigade would have let that stop them.

---

1. *2000 Years of Charismatic Christianity,* Eddie L. Hyatt, Charisma House, Lake Mary, Florida, p. 112.

2. *Pilgrims and Patriots,* Eddie L. Hyatt, Hyatt Press, PO Box 3877, Grapevine, TX, pp. 108, 109.

3. *The Founders' Bible,* Signature Historian David Barton, Shiloh Road Publishers, 4680 Calle Norte, Newbury Park, CA 91320. ISBN 978-1-61871-001-7, p. 558.

4. *The Light and The Glory,* Marshall and Manuel, Revell Division of Baker Publishing, Grand Rapids, MI, p. 320.

5. *Rev. Jonas Clark and the Battle of Lexington April, 1775.* Article excerpted from *America's Providential History* by Mark Beliles and Stephen McDowell. Order from the *Providence Foundation Store.*

6. Ibid.

7. *The Light and The Glory,* Marshall and Manuel, p. 342.

8. Ibid. p. 342.

9. *Pilgrims and Patriots,* Hyatt, pp. 118, 119.

10. *The Founder's Bible,* p. 678.

CHAPTER 13

COLONIAL MINISTERS AND THE DECLARATION OF INDEPENDENCE

There is not a right asserted in the Declaration of Independence which had not been discussed by the New England clergy before 1763."[1]

D avid Barton, Founder and President of *Wallbuilders,* was one of the leaders of the tour I was privileged to take. (Which I am sure is one of the "God dots" in my life.) He is the "Signature Historian" of *The Founders' Bible.* This *New American Standard* translation of the Bible is richly interspersed with historical documents and facts about our country's founding.

If you've ever heard David speak, you know how he can expound almost "fast and furiously" upon the evidence of God in the foundation of The United States of America. His own massive library of over 100,000 original source documents from the Founding Era surpasses any private collection and vies with those of some museums. It seems like, when you hear David, that he has memorized the documents which reveal the place of God in our Founding Fathers' hearts and pens.

For you who really want to know the truth of the matter, I highly suggest you get the 2194-page *The Founders' Bible.*

INDEPENDENCE

The following is from a section in *The Founders' Bible* entitled *Birthplace of American Independence, Pastor John Wise and the Womb of Liberty.*[2]

> Perhaps you've read or heard that the main premises of the Declaration of Independence, such as "all men are created equal," were derived from the Enlightenment, or the Age of Reason, and have no biblical origin... But if we study the origin and meaning of the famous phrases in the Declaration, we discover otherwise.
>
> When President Calvin Coolidge gave a speech in 1926 on the 150th anniversary of the Declaration, he attributed the meaning of its key phrases to two books published in 1710 and 1717 by John Wise, the Congregational pastor of Ipswich, Massachusetts. Coolidge called these books a "textbook of liberty for our Revolutionary fathers."

On the web site of *National Black Robe Regiment* I found the following:

> As early as 1687, the Rev. Wise was already teaching that "taxation without representation is tyranny,"[3] the "consent of the governed" was the foundation of government,"[4] and that "every man must be acknowledged equal to every man."[5]
>
> In 1772 with the Revolution on the horizon, two of Wise's works were reprinted by leading patriots and

the Sons of Liberty to refresh America's understanding of the core Biblical principles of government.[6] (The first printing sold so fast that a quick second reprint was quickly issued.) Significantly, many of the specific points made by Wise in that work subsequently appeared four years later in the very language of the Declaration of Independence. As historian Benjamin Morris affirmed in 1864:

[S]ome of the most glittering sentences in the immortal Declaration of Independence are almost literal quotations from this [1772 reprinted] essay of John Wise. ...It was used as a political text-book in the great struggle for freedom.[7]

---

1. *The New England Clergy and the American Revolution,* Alice M. Baldwin, New York, NY: Frederick Ungar, 1958, p. 170.

2. *The Founders' Bible,* Shiloh Road Publishers, 4680 Calle Norte, Newbury Park, CA. p. 1964. Adapted with permission from the July 2011 Plymouth Rock Foundation -News article written by Dr. Paul Jehle, Executive Director of the foundation.

3. *The Other Cape,* Linda Stewart, American Heritage (at: http://www.americanheritage.com/articles/magazine/ah/2001/2/2001_2_50.shtml)

4. *Seedtime of the Republic,* Clinton Rossiter, New York: Harcourt, Brace and Co., 1953, p. 219.

5. *"Top Ipswich Patriots"* by Thomas Franklin Waters & Mrs. Eunice Whitney Farley Felten, Lord Family Album, 1927 (at: http://www.bwlord.com/Ipswich/Waters/TwoPatriots/JohnWise.htm).

6. Ibid.

7. *A Vindication of the Government of New England Churches: and the Churches' Quarrel Espoused,* John Wise, Boston: Congregational Board of Publication, 1860, pp. xx-xxi, "Introductory Remarks" by Rev. J. S. Clark. See also B.F. Morris, Christian Life and Character of the Civil Institutions of the United States, Developed in the Official and Historical Annals of the Republic, Philadelphia: George W. Childs, 1864, p. 341.

CHAPTER 14

PRAYER AND THE MAKING OF THE NATION

Oh! thus be it ever, when freemen shall stand
Between their loved home and the war's desolation!
Blest with victory and peace, may the heav'n rescued land
Praise the Power that hath made and preserved us a nation.
Then conquer we must, when our cause it is just,
And this be our motto: "In God is our trust."
And the star spangled banner in triumph shall wave
O'er the land of the free and the home of the brave!
(The Star Spangled Banner, Verse 4)

The purpose of this book is not to attempt an in-depth coverage of the hand of God in the struggle for independence. For more complete accounts, I recommend the books I have used as sources.

Our purpose is to discover the Awakenings this nation has known as God both "made" and "preserved" us a nation. To discover what brought about those Awakenings. And to discover how we can work with God in realizing His destiny for America. To do this we examine history.

THE FOUNDING FATHERS

The Great Awakening affected our Founding Fathers. Some directly, such as Patrick Henry who gave the famous "Give me Liberty or Give me death," speech at the Virginia Convention.

> Henry acquired his deep biblicism in part from his parents, and in part from his autodidactic education in which the Bible took a central role. But as a child he was also introduced to religious controversy of a kind that was seen in many parts of the colonies. Henry came from a traditional Anglican family, and he remained an Anglican (or Episcopalian, after the Revolution) throughout his life. However, in the 1740s and 1750s Patrick Henry's family found itself in the middle of the first serious uprising against traditional authorities in colonial America, a series of religious revivals commonly referred to as the Great Awakening.
>
> ...Patrick Henry's mother Sarah. Despite the fact that her husband was an Anglican vestryman, ...found Presbyterian pastor Samuel Davies's preaching irresistible, and she joined his maverick congregation. Henry family tradition holds that Sarah would take twelve-year-old Patrick to the evangelical Presbyterian meetings, and require him to repeat the biblical text and essence of the sermon to her... Like numerous populist politicians who have followed him, Henry adapted the evangelical style to politics. He later insisted that Samuel Davies not only delivered finer sermons than any preacher he ever encountered, but that Davies was the "greatest orator he ever heard."[1]

THE FIRST CONTINENTAL CONGRESS
OPENED WITH PRAYER

The Great Awakening had brought a sense of unity to the American colonists. The tyrannical acts of King George III drove them to a unified response. Delegates from the thirteen colonies met in Carpenter's Hall in Philadelphia on September 5, 1774.

Eddie Hyatt's *Pilgrims and Patriots* gives an excellent account of how they began with prayer:[2]

> This Congress would not have been possible apart from the Great Awakening, which had broken down social and denominational barriers. This became obvious at the first meeting... when it was proposed that they begin their deliberations with prayer. Two delegates opposed the motion on the grounds that they were such a diverse religious group, including Anglicans, Puritans, Presbyterians and Quakers, that it would be impossible for them to pray together.
>
> Samuel Adams, a Puritan from Boston who had been impacted by the Awakening, arose and said that he was not a bigoted man and that he could join in prayer with any person of piety and virtue who loved his country. He went on to say that, although he was a stranger to Philadelphia, he had heard of an Anglican minister, a Rev. Jabob Dusche, who was such a man, and he proposed that they invite him to come and lead them in prayer. Adams' proposal was approved and Dusche was asked to preside over a time of Bible reading and prayer.
>
> As the elderly, grey-haired Dusche stood before the Congress, he began by reading the entire 35th Psalm, which powerfully impacted everyone present. It is a prayer of David for deliverance and begins

with the words, *Plead my cause O LORD with those who strive against me; fight against those who fight against me.* The Psalm ends with praise for God's deliverance.

As the Psalm was read, a unique sense of God's presence filled the room and tears flowed from many eyes. John Adams wrote to his wife, Abigail, of the impact of the Bible reading and prayer on the delegates. He wrote,

> Who can realize the emotions with which they turned imploringly to heaven for divine interposition and aid. It was enough to melt a heart of stone. I never saw a greater effect upon an audience. It seems as if heaven had ordained the Psalm to be read that day. I saw tears gush into the eyes of the old, grave pacific Quakers of Philadelphia. I must beg you to read that Psalm.[3]

Prayer continued to be a daily and vital part of the proceedings of the Continental Congresses... During the Revolutionary War, the Congress issued no less than fifteen separate calls for special days of prayer and fasting.

"THE FATHER OF OUR COUNTRY" A MAN OF PRAYER

Washington was a man of prayer, and he learned it from his mother. Online, I found William J. Johnson's book, *George Washington the Christian.*[4] The following quotes are from that enlightening book written almost one hundred years ago, i.e. before the rise of revisionist history.

In November, 1753, then twenty-one years of age,

Washington was commissioned by Governor Din-widdie, of Virginia, to be the bearer of dispatches to the French commander St. Pierre. He called to see his mother and explained the nature of his mission. "With her farewell kiss she bade him 'remember that God only is our sure trust. To Him I commend you.'"[5]

As he left... his mother's parting charge was, "My son, neglect not the duty of secret prayer." Never did a mother give better advice to her son, and never did a son more conscientiously follow it.[6]

The evidence that he followed that advice is well documented. I chose just a couple from the midst of the war he commanded, and again these are sources Johnson quoted:

March 6, 1776, General Washington issued at Cambridge the following order:

Thursday, the 7th instant, being set apart by the honorable the Legislature of this Province as a day of fasting, prayer, and humiliation, "to implore the Lord and Giver of all victory to pardon our manifold sins and wickedness, and that it would please Him to bless the Continental arms with His divine favor and protection," all officers and soldiers are strictly enjoined to pay all due reverence and attention on that day to the sacred duties to the Lord of hosts for His mercies already received, and for those blessings which our holiness and uprightness of life can alone encourage us to hope through His mercy to obtain.[7]

In his answer to an address from the General Assembly of Massachusetts, following evacuation of Boston by the British, March 17, 1776, he closed:

And it being effected without the blood of our soldiers and fellow-citizens must be ascribed to the interposition of that Providence which has manifest-ly appeared in our behalf through the whole of this important struggle, as well as to the measures for bringing about the happy event.

May that Being who is powerful to save, and in whose hands is the fate of nations, look down with an eye of tender pity and compassion upon the whole of the United Colonies may He continue to smile upon their counsels and arms, and crown them with success, whilst employed in the cause of virtue and mankind. May this distressed colony and its capital, and every part of this wide extended con-tinent, through His divine favor, be restored to more than their former lustre [sic] and once happy state, and have peace, liberty, and safety secured upon a solid, permanent, and lasting foundation.[8]

When Mary commended her son to "God our only sure trust," her words of faith, and her son's prayer life, I believe, gave God the channel through which George Washington was supernaturally protected. If the biblical Hall of Fame of the heroes of faith in God has been added to in Heaven's books, then surely their names are written therein. (Hebrews 11.)

Evidence after evidence of divine intervention in the Continental Army's victories show the hand of God. George Washington was preserved and prepared to head that army.

Entering the Virginia militia as a young officer, Wash-ington distinguished himself in combat during the French and Indian Wars. The campaigns in which he served included the Battle of the Monongahe-la, fought on July 9, 1755. In this action the British forces under General Edward Braddock were deci-mated, with the commander himself being killed.

Fifteen years after this battle, Washington and his lifelong friend Dr. Craik were exploring and surveying the wilderness territory in the Western Reserve. Near the junction of the Kanawha and Ohio Rivers, a band of Indians came to them with an interpreter. The leader of the band was an old and venerable chief who wished to have words with Washington. A council fire was kindled, and this is what the chief said:

> I am a chief and ruler over my tribes. My influence extends to the waters of the great lakes, and to the far blue mountains. I have traveled a long and weary path, that I might see the young warrior of the great battle. It was on the day when the white man's blood mixed with the streams of our forest, that I first beheld this chief. I called to my young men and said, "Mark yon tall and daring warrior? He is not of the red-coat tribe — he hath an Indian's wisdom, and his warriors fight as we do — himself alone is exposed. Quick let your aim be certain, and he dies." Our rifles were leveled, rifles which, but for him, knew not how to miss... 'Twas all in vain; a power mightier far than we shielded him from harm. He cannot die in battle. I am old, and soon shall be gathered to the great council fire of my fathers in the land of shades, but ere I go, there is something that bids me speak in the voice of prophecy: Listen! The Great Spirit protects that man, and guides his destinies — he will become the chief of nations, and a people yet unborn will hail him as the founder of a mighty empire.[9]

Confirmation of this episode can be found in Bancroft's multi-volume definitive nineteenth-century history of the United States. At that same battle, according to other sources as well as Washington's journal, the twenty-three-year-old colonel had two horses shot out from under him and four musket balls pass through his coat. There was nothing wrong with the Indians' marksmanship.

"Death," wrote Washington to his brother, Jack, "was leveling my companions on every side of me, but by the all-powerful dispensations of Providence, I have been protected."[10] This conviction was further shared by Samuel Davies, the famous Virginia Presbyterian evangelist, who wrote, "To the public I point out that heroic youth [Washington]... whom I cannot but hope Providence has preserved in so signal a manner for some important service to his country."

This was God's man, chosen for America's hour of greatest crisis.[11]

THE NECESSITY OF PRAYER

John Wesley famously said something like this, "It seems that God can do nothing for mankind except a man asks Him."

I really shouldn't attempt to explain why this is so in a few paragraphs, but here goes. Just in a nutshell.

Adam, was given a six-day work week, a day being as a thousand years and a thousand years as a day. (Psalm 90:3, 2 Peter 3:8; The Talmud, Tractate Sanhedrin, Folio 97a.) Adam was given dominion over this planet. Legally, but not morally, he handed over dominion to the adversary of God, Satan. Satan usurped Adam's authority. The New Testament calls Satan "the god of this world," "the prince of the powers (authorities) of the air." (2 Cor. 4:4, Eph. 2:2.)

The prayers of a covenant man or woman penetrate the "air" where Satan has set up his task force. Prayer gives God the legal right to move in mankind's behalf. To bring things from the Unseen realm into the Seen.

When Adam's lease is over, The Day of the Lord will come.

Until then, someone with a legal right to being on this earth, someone who was born into earth in the legal way (Satan is an illegal alien) can pray in line with the Word of God and expect God to answer.

Thank God, those through whom God brought The Great Awakening, and our Founding Fathers, knew the value and necessity of prayer.

1. *Evangelism in Patrick Henry's "Liberty or Death" Speech,* Thomas Kidd, Found online at WE'RE HISTORY.
2. *Pilgrims and Patriots,* Eddie L. Hyatt, Hyatt Press. pp. 121, 122.
3. *On Two Wings: Humble Faith and Common Sense at the American Founding,* Michael Novak, San Francisco: Encounter, 2002, p. 14.
4. *George Washington the Christian,* William J. Johnson, The Abingdon Press, NY, Cincinnati, Copyright 1919.
5. *The Story of Mary Washington,* Marion Harland, 1892 p. 87.
6. *The Writings of George Washington,* Jared Sparks, 12 Vols., 1837-7.
7. *The Cambridge of 1776,* with the diary of Dorothy Dudley, 1876.
8. Sparks, Vol. IX.
9. *George Washington the Christian,* Johnson, p. 36.
10. This note and the following are from Bancroft, *History,* vol. 4, 190.
11. *The Light and the Glory,* Marshall and Manuel, pp. 360, 361.

Chapter 15

The Second Great Awakening (1800-1840)

Praise the Power that hath made and preserved us a nation.
(The Star Spangled Banner)

The pattern of our Gracious Lord's outpouring of His Spirit in subsequent Awakenings, was that the previous outpouring would wane, there would be a national backsliding into a darkness and a state of sleep that required an Awakening. The Lord would stir His people to pray. And in answer to fervent prayer, He would send another Awakening.

The Second Great Awakening (1800 – 1840)

That was the case as the nineteenth century dawned. Eddie L. Hyatt writes:

> A generation had come of age that knew little of the revival that had swept the nation sixty years earlier... Negative influences from the French Revolution were penetrating American society, and deism was at its peak of popularity. All of this resulted in a rise in profanity, drunkenness, gambling and lewdness.
> The General Assembly of the Presbyterian

Church circulated a pastoral letter declaring they were "filled with concern and awful dread" at conditions they beheld on every hand. They expressed the solemn conviction "that the eternal God has a controversy with this nation." This concern prompted fervent prayer that precipitated a national spiritual awakening beginning on the East Coast around 1800 and spreading to the western frontier.[1]

If you are a student of revivals and awakenings, it is to this period that belong: Revival fires in Kentucky under Pastor James McGready. Barton Stone and The Cane Ridge Revival. Campmeetings among Presbyterians, Baptists, and Methodists with thousands attending.

Hyatt writes, "Peter Cartwright, a Methodist preacher, stated, 'The work went on and spread almost in every direction gathering additional force till our country seemed all coming to God.'

"The Spirit of God prevailed over infidelity and deism, and the religious character of the United States was assured for generations to come."[2]

A FAMILY LETTER

I am among those "generations to come" who benefitted from The Second Great Awakening. I remember very well my Great Grandmother born Fannie Otie Womack. Her father was Larkin Womack. His mother was Catherine Blankenship Womack.

Catherine Womack lived in Lynchburg, Virginia when she wrote a series of letters (1835-1842) to her son, William, who had moved to Sangamon County, Illinois. The following is an excerpt from her letter dated, August 16, 1842. I have left the spelling as she wrote:

> ...your brother Larkin. He was veary low with the fever... You must expect my dear William that my dear Larkin was most gone...he lay sick, which I think was about six weeks confinement to the house, but the Lord was pleased to raise him from the bed of affliction and I saw him last Thursday evening. He was in good health of body and of soul too apparently. He is a veary pious youth and if you hear him preaching the Gospel you need not be at all alarmed... He has commenced going to school...and seems to take such delight in the ways and worship of God. And John is still going on in religious ways. And, O my William do you not think that a great comfort to me? And would it not be a greater one still to hear in your next letter you embraced religion? You say in your letter you nor your wife had not profest religion, and you have regular meetings with the Methodists, Baptists, and Presbiterians.
>
> Well, my son, so you and your wife attend to preaching and do you wish to get religion? Then if you do get down on your knees and pray to God to have mercy on you and show you your sinful state that you are in by nature, for ye must be born again... Oh, my William, read the Bible a great deal and attend to preaching and if there is any revival out with you, write me word in your next letter and I pray you my dear son and daughter-in-law, be you both at the altar that the people of God may pray for your dear souls...

I too am grateful that the Lord raised up Larkin. Otherwise you would not be reading this book.

1.   *2000 Years of Charismatic Christianity,* Eddie L. Hyatt, Charisma House, A Strang Company, Lake Mary, FL, p. 113.
2.   Ibid. pp. 116, 117.

Chapter 16

An Awakening of Prayer

Praise the Power that hath made and preserved us a nation.
(The Star Spangled Banner)

Charles G. Finney led a move of God that met the definition of an Awakening. It affected the whole of society. Someone has called Finney's memoirs of that move as, "perhaps the most remarkable account of the manifestations of the Holy Spirit's power since apostolic days. It is crowded with accounts of spiritual outpourings which remind one of the Day of Pentecost."[1]

I'm not going to go into the depths that Awakening deserves, however, except to see how it affected the Awakening that surely "preserved" us a nation just before The Civil War.

Again, I highly recommend a book which covers so well the Finney outpouring as well as revivals and awakenings in America and around the world. It is *Revival Fire* by Wesley Duewel.[2]

Duewel declares that Finney's "revival campaign in Rochester in 1856 prepared the way of the Lord for the mighty movement of revival that swept America in 1857."[3]

When Finney listed the "striking characteristics" of revivals, the first he mentioned was: "The prevalence of a mighty Spirit of prevailing prayer."[4]

A movement of prevailing prayer is what the Lord used to lead us into the Awakening, which I believe, preserved us a nation through the judgment of The Civil War. Slavery was indeed judged. But the Republic was saved.

The New York City Prayer Meetings

In 1858, Talbot W. Chambers, as pastor of the North Dutch Church, Fulton Street, NY, wrote the account of the noon prayer meetings that began there. The Fulton Street Church stood near where the World Trade Center subsequently stood — between West Street and Greenwich, crossing at Fulton.

The church building dated back to pre-Revolutionary War days. Its first immediate environs were homes of families of Dutch descent. But by 1858, Chambers wrote:

> But of late years the tendency has been quite the other way. The rapid and constant growth of the city demanded ever-increasing accommodations for its trade and commerce. Streets once filled with the families of substantial citizens were invaded by shops and warehouses... [dwellings] were replaced by stately blocks adapted solely to business purposes... the attendance at the North Church... was reduced almost to a skeleton. Yet there was no decrease... in the population immediately around the old edifice. But... the character of the people was greatly changed. Instead of the staid, settled families

of fixed principles... there was now a mixed multi-
tude... from every part of Europe, and some even
from the remoter regions of Asia. The greater part
brought with them no habits of reverence or worship...[5]

The church board decided to hire someone to reach the new
population — a lay missionary. They hired Jeremiah Lanphier, a middle-aged businessman. Described as, "tall, with a
pleasant face, an affectionate manner, and indomitable energy and perseverance; a good singer, gifted in prayer and
exhortation, a welcome guest to any house, shrewd and en-
dowed with much tact, and common sense."[6]

Lanphier worked from dawn to dark visiting people in
the offices and shops and factories, with some little results.
He grew weary. But he discovered that if he took an hour in
the middle of the day to pray at the church he was revitalized
spiritually and physically. Chambers writes:

Waiting upon the Lord, he renewed his strength;
calling upon God, he was answered. His own soul
was cheered and refreshed, and he was enabled to
set forth upon his daily rounds with a quickened
sense of the Divine favour, and a heartier assurance
that his labour would not be in vain in the Lord.

This fresh, personal experience of the blessed-
ness and power of prayer suggested to Mr. Lanphier's mind that there might be others, especially those
engaged in business, to whom it would be equally
pleasant and profitable to retire for a short period
from secular engagements and engage in devotional
exercises.

Since the normal practice of the many different kinds of businesses in the area was to take the hour from twelve to one o'clock for "rest and refreshment," Lanphier decided to print a handbill to advertise a meeting at that hour. The handbill read:

> DAILY
> PRAYER MEETING
> From 12 to 1 o'clock.
> —STOP—
> 5, 10, or 20 Minutes,
> or the whole hour,
> AS YOUR TIME ADMITS.

The first meeting was scheduled for Wednesday, September 23, 1857 in a third floor room in the Consistory building. Precisely at noon Jeremiah Lanphier took his seat and prayed as he waited to see if anyone would come. Thirty minutes passed before the footsteps of one person were heard climbing the stairs. Soon another appeared, and another, until the first gathering numbered six.

On the next Wednesday, September 30th, twenty men gathered. On October 7th, forty were present.

It was decided to make the meeting a daily affair. And the place of the meeting changed to the second floor.

There was unity and harmony from the start. People shared prayer requests and gave testimony to prayers answered. Rules were established and signs posted:

PRAYERS & EXHORTATIONS
Not to exceed 5 minutes,
in order to give all an opportunity.
NOT MORE than 2 CONSECUTIVE
PRAYERS OR EXHORTATIONS
NO CONTROVERTED POINTS
— DISCUSSED —

Another sign read: *Brethren are earnestly requested to adhere to the 5 minute rule.*

Within a few weeks the place was packed. Those in attendance felt "an awesome sense of God's Presence." And pastors from other churches who attended the Fulton Street meeting began prayer meetings across the city.

Wesley Duewel reports:

> Soon the places where the meetings were held were overcrowded. Men and women young and old of all denominations met and prayed together without distinctions. The meetings abounded with love for Christ, love for fellow Christians, love for prayer, and love of witnessing. Those in attendance felt an awesome sense of God's presence. They prayed for specific people, expected answers and obtained answers.[7]

ANSWERED PRAYER

Reverend Talbot Chambers wrote his book at the time of the meetings and supplied specific accounts of answered prayer. Here are a few of those:

> **A father ... had three sons** in distant and different parts of the country, all unconverted. He brought them to the Meeting as subjects of prayer. They were prayed for as only those who believe can pray. What has been the consequence? Three letters have been received from these three sons, who have not communicated with each other — each giving an account of his own conversion.

> **In a similar case, the father brought before the Meeting the welfare of his son far away in the distant Pacific;** and in accordance with his request, fervent prayers were offered. In due season the son returned home, and it was found that he had been converted not only in mid-ocean, but also about the very time that he was made a subject of prayer.
>
> In stating this fact, the father said, "I determined at the time to note down the date of the prayer meeting at which my son was remembered... Away at that distance, God called his attention to religion, convinced him of his guilt, led him to Christ, and the very first thing he had to tell me on landing was, what the Lord had done for his soul. He knew nothing of our prayer meeting.

> **On the 7th of July last, a lady tarried after the Prayer Meeting** to say that she wished to have a request written, to be presented next day for prayer for the conversion of her husband in Wisconsin...
>
> She was present, and heard the prayer offered.

She then went to stay two weeks at Yonkers. After the lapse of that time, she returned home to Wisconsin. On arriving home, her husband, said, "I have set up family worship since you went away."

"Ah! When did you commence?"

"Some time back."

"Well, I had your case made a subject of prayer at the Union Prayer Meeting, Fulton Street, when I was in New York."

"Oh, did you, and on what day was it?"

"It was on the 8th of July."

"Why, that was the very day on which God had mercy on my soul!"

This lady has lately written a letter to a friend here, full of grateful acknowledgments, through whom these facts have been communicated to the Meeting. "Before they call I will answer, and while they are yet speaking I will hear."[8]

THE POWER OF PRAYER
AND THE
POWER OF THE PRESS

Talbot reports that the press picked up the New York City meetings and covered their progress:

> ...the daily press of the city had its attention drawn to a topic now become one of universal interest. Reporters were dispatched to the various prayer meetings, and "the Progress of the Revival" became a standing head of intelligence in several widely circulated journals. Remarkable cases of awakening were detailed at length, and all items of religious information were eagerly seized to gratify the presumed demands of readers.[9]

No doubt, this attention, as well as word of mouth brought more and more people. The churches holding meetings likewise became crowded. A theater was opened for meetings and people lined up for an hour and a half before time to begin. Hundreds were turned away.

The meetings spread to other cities and the Presence of God attended them as well. Talbot shares that "the custom was introduced of exchanging dispatches with each other by magnetic telegraph. One of these, received from Philadelphia, is inserted as an illustration."[10]

> Philadelphia, Saturday, March 18, 12:15 P.M.
> To Mr. W. Wetmore, Fulton Street Meeting:
> Jayne's Hall Daily Prayer Meeting is crowded, upwards of three thousand present; with one mind and heart they glorify our Father in heaven, for the mighty work he is doing in our city and country in the building up of saints and the conversion of sinners. The Lord hath done great things for us, whence joy to us is brought...
> Geo. H. Stuart, *Chairman of the Meeting.*

That reminds me of what the Bible says about the City of Samaria at the outpouring that came when Philip preached Christ unto them, *"And there was great joy in that city"* (Acts 8:8). Another Scripture that comes to mind is, *"So mightily grew the word of God and prevailed"* (Acts 19:20).

The Prayer Meetings grew and the Holy Spirit prevailed.

PRAYER AND POWER
FAR AND WIDE

Wesley Duewel reports the "Prayer Meeting Fervor" with a fervor of his own that comes across in his book.

> Almost simultaneously noon prayer meetings sprang up all across America in Boston, Baltimore, Washington D.C., Richmond, Charleston, Savannah, Mobile, New Orleans, Vicksburg, Memphis, St. Louis, Pittsburgh, Cincinnati, Chicago, and in a multitude of other cities, towns, and in rural areas. By the end of the fourth month, prayer fervor burned intensely across the nation...
>
> America had entered a new period of faith and prayer. Educated and uneducated, rich and poor, business leaders and common workmen — all prayed, believed, and received answers to prayer. Even the President of the United States, Franklin Pierce, attended many of the noon prayer meetings. This was not a revival of powerful preaching. This was a movement of earnest, powerful, prevailing prayer.
>
> All people wanted was a place to pray... In some towns, nearly the entire population became saved ... *a spirit of prayer occupied the land, as though the church had suddenly discovered its real power.* [The emphasis is mine! B.B.]
>
> *The Presbyterian Magazine* reported that as of May there had been fifty thousand converts of the revival. In February, a New York Methodist magazine reported a total of eight thousand conversions in Methodist meetings in one week. The Louisville daily paper reported seventeen thousand Baptist conversions in three weeks during the month of March. And according to a June statement, the conversion

figures stood at 96,216 — and still counting.

...For six to eight weeks during the height of the revival, some fifty thousand people were converted weekly. The average for two whole years was ten thousand new converts joining the churches each week.

The Washington National Intelligencer reported that in several New England towns not a single unconverted person could be found. State after state reported sweeping revival...

Of the thirty million people living in the United States, nearly two million were won to Christ during the revival. The moral change was so great across the country that the Louisville, Kentucky, daily paper reported that the millennium had arrived.[11]

Imagine that! Thinking the Millennium had arrived. I believe that in the next Great Awakening we will think that the Lord is soon to arrive!

1.   *Revival Fire,* Wesley Duewel, Zondervan, Grand Rapids, MI.
2.   Ibid. p. 92.
3.   *The Memoirs of Charles G. Finney,* Garth M. Rosell and Richard A.G. Dupuis, ed., Zondervan, Grand Rapids, MI, 1989, p. 80.
4.   *The New York City Noon Prayer Meeting, A Simple Prayer Meeting that Changed the World,* Talbot W. Chambers, Published by Campus Renewal Ministries, 2009, 2421 San Antonio St., Suite B, Austin TX. Reprinted with permission from Global Harvest Ministries, Colorado Springs, CO, p. 25.
5.   Ibid. p. 29.
6.   *Revival Fires,* Wesley Duewel, pp. 128, 129.
7.   *NYC Noon Prayer Meeting.* pp. 86, 87.
8.   Ibid. p. 47.
9.   Ibid. p. 47.
10. Ibid. p. 48.
11. *Revival Fires,* Wesley Duewel, pp. 129-131.

CHAPTER 17

GOD PRESERVED US A NATION

Praise the Power that hath made and preserved us a nation.
(The Star Spangled Banner)

The United States could have judged itself on the matter of slavery; but since it did not, it brought judgment upon itself. Yet in the judgment, God remembered mercy. He stirred America to prayer, allowing Him to send another Great Awakening.

Unified by the Spirit of Prayer the nation was fortified to escape the complete destruction the war could have brought. (I so believe that it can and will happen again — another Great Awakening. We can know a unity in the Spirit of God that can ward off the division the enemy has designed. And only this can — only an Awakening to God — will save America.)

Duewel writes, "The fourth great awakening was above all a revival of unity."[1]

THE GLORY OF GOD'S PRESENCE

The Glory of God is the Presence of God manifested. In the

Bible it was seen as a cloud, fire, smoke, etc. Just a very few exemplary scriptures are: Exodus 24:16-17; 40:34-35; 2 Chronicles 5:14; 7:1-3.

God's Glorious Presence was evidenced in every move of God meeting the definition of an Awakening.

> A canopy of holy and awesome revival influence — in reality the presence of the Holy Spirit — seemed to hang like an invisible cloud over many parts of the United States, especially over the eastern seaboard. At times this cloud of God's presence even seemed to extend out to sea. Those on ships approaching the east coast at times felt a solemn, holy influence, even one hundred miles away, without even knowing what was happening in America.
>
> Revival began aboard one ship before it reached the coast. People on board began to feel the presence of God and a sense of their own sinfulness. The Holy Spirit convicted them, and they began to pray. As the ship neared the harbor, the captain signaled, "Send a minister."
>
> Another small commercial ship arrived in port with the captain, and every member of the crew converted in the last 150 miles. Ship after ship arrived with the same story: both passengers and crew were suddenly convicted of sin and turned to Christ before they reached the American coast.
>
> The battleship North Carolina was anchored in New York harbor as a naval receiving ship. More than a thousand young men were on board. Four Christians agreed to meet together for prayer and knelt on the lower deck. The Spirit of God so filled their hearts with joy that they broke into song. Ungodly men on the top deck heard the singing, looked down, and saw the boys kneeling. They began running down the stairs, mocking and jeering. The con-

victing power of the Holy Spirit so gripped them that by the time they reached the bottom deck they fell on their knees and began crying for mercy.

Strong men who were deep in sin were broken down by the Spirit's power and knelt humbly in penitence and faith. Night after night the sailors prayed, and hundreds were converted on the ship. Ministers were sent for... the battleship became a mighty center of revival.[2]

From 1857-1859 the Fourth Great Awakening spread across the continent. What began in the nation's cities spread throughout the towns and villages and even in the fields across America.

Jayne's Hall in Philadelphia expanded its meeting space to accommodate six thousand people. "For months multitudes of churches opened every evening for prayer."[3]

IN THE NORTH
AND
IN THE SOUTH

The cities and the countryside where the revival spread were in all parts of America.

Many of my ancestors lived in the South. A few in the North. Thank God, the outpouring knew no lines of division.

Because of the bitter tensions of the Civil War and the slavery issue, for a time it seemed that the southern states would not be as powerfully influenced by the revival as the northern ones had been... An unusually powerful revival broke out among the southern troops stationed around Richmond, Virginia in the autumn of 1861. It began in the hospitals among the wounded men and then spread into the camps as these men returned to active duty. Prayer meetings were organized and hundreds converted. The movement spread rapidly throughout the army, reaching the troops of Tennessee and Arkansas.

Revival was encouraged by Generals Robert E. Lee and Thomas J. "Stonewall" Jackson, who were well known as devout Christians. By the mid-summer of 1863 the revival had spread through all the Confederate armies, and thousands of men had been converted. Chaplains and lay missionaries went out among the troops, preaching and distributing tracts and dealing personally with hungry hearts. By the end of the war at least 150,000 soldiers had been converted, and more than a third of all of the southern troops had become praying men. The revival among the southern troops was primarily a revival of prayer, as the earlier revival in the North had been. While the best estimates are that 6.6 percent of the entire population of the United States was converted during the revival, the percentage among the southern troops was 21 percent.[4]

Think of how many soldiers on both sides stepped out into Eternity. Thank God for his merciful outpouring that preserved not only the nation, but its people.

I have already introduced you to Larkin Womack. His wife gave birth to my Great Grandmother, Fannie Otie Womack, in 1860 in Richmond, Virginia. Larkin's life was not only saved from a lengthy illness in his youth, but through many Civil War battles. My grandmother was the family's eighth child. I have tried to imagine what it must have been like for her mother.

My Grandpa Coday's father, William F. Coday, was one

brother in a family of fighting age boys when the Civil War caused great division in the state of Missouri where they lived. Their father said to his sons, when they were facing the unimaginable decision as to which side to fight for, "We'll stay with the flag, boys."

How merciful is our God. He visited both the North and the South in the Awakening. He stirred up people to pray and anointed their efforts in prayer so that He could preserve us a nation.

1.   *Revival Fire,* Wesley Duewel. p. 132.
2.   Ibid. pp. 133, 134.
3.   Ibid. p. 135.
4.   Ibid. pp. 135, 136.

CHAPTER 18

THE AUTHORITY OF THE BELIEVER

Praise the Power that hath made and preserved us a nation.
(The Star Spangled Banner)

At this writing, our nation is embroiled in deep divisions. I could name them, but you know what they are.

Of course, humans know differences of opinions, thoughts and ideas that are common to humankind and not deadly. Those in which we can agree to disagree. But then there are those that can produce a division that would ultimately destroy. These, I believe, are satanically driven.

I sincerely believe that there is a divine destiny for America. As we wrote about in Chapter Two of this book, God brought America forth at His appointed time and established her borders (Acts 17:24, 26). If that is so, then the enemy of God would bring all his powers against America's success. Spiritual problems can only be solved with spiritual solutions.

> **Eph. 6:12** For we wrestle not against flesh and blood, but against principalities, against powers, against the rulers of the darkness of this world, against spiritual wickedness in high *places.*

> **2 Cor. 10:4** (For the weapons of our warfare *are* not car-
> nal, but mighty through God to the pulling down of strong
> holds;)

Carnal means "of the flesh." Natural weapons, in other words. The greatest weapon we can wield against the darkness arrayed against this nation is our God-given authority over the kingdom of darkness.

THE AUTHORITY OF THE BELIEVER

To triumph over the dark forces assigned against our nation, the Body of Christ can and must exercise her authority over them. This is so important that I am borrowing heavily from my book, *How You Can Pray in The End of Days.*[1] And in that book, I quoted from the marvelous book by John A. MacMillan, a missionary to China and the Philippians entitled, *The Authority of the Believer.*[2]

John A. MacMillan's book contains such spiritual treasure that we bought the rights to publish it. The powerful message begins in the book's preface:

> The rapidly approaching end of the age is witnessing
> a tremendous increase in the activity of the powers
> of darkness... To meet the situation the Church of
> Christ needs a new conception of prayer. The urgent
> call is for men and women, wholly yielded to the
> Lord, whose eyes have been enlightened to see *the
> ministry in the heavenlies* to which they have been
> called. Such believers... may in union with the great
> Head of the Body, exercise an authority to which the
> powers of the air must give place wherever chal-
> lenged.[3]

MacMillan departed earth in 1956. How much greater now is the increase of the activity of the powers of darkness.

This increase is primarily due to the fact that Satan sees his time is short and he is struggling to survive (Revelation 12:12). He well knows that the Body of Christ has an authority over him that he must obey. Our challenge is to get the Body of Christ to awaken to it and exercise it. This awakening is a vital part to our knowing an Awakening to God that will save America.

TWO GREEK WORDS

First, the King James Version of the Bible uses one English word, *power,* to translate several different Greek words. The two of most interest to us here are: *dunamis* and *exousia. The Companion Bible,* Appendix 172, defines their meanings under the heading "The Synonymous Words for 'Power'":[4]

> 1. **dunamis** = inherent power; the power of reproducing itself: from which we have Eng. dynamics, dynamo, &c. See Acts 1.8.

> 5. **exousia** = authority, or, delegated power; the liberty and right to put forth power. See, e.g., John 1.12.

A police officer does not have the *dunamis* to stop heavy traffic. Human physical strength is no match for a motor vehicle. But when a uniformed officer holds up his or her hand, all traffic stops. The authority, *exousia,* behind the badge demands compliance.

One scripture in which the KJV uses *power* to translate both words is Luke 10:19. I have inserted the Greek words.

> **Luke 10:19** Behold, I give unto you **power** *[exousia]* to tread on serpents and scorpions, and over all the **power** *[dunamis]* of the enemy: and nothing shall by any means hurt you.

The seventy, to whom Jesus spoke directly, did not have the *dunamis* power to dominate the demons of the kingdom of darkness. But Jesus delegated to them the authority *(exousia)* to dominate Satan's cohorts.

Authority is delegated power.

Jesus defeated Satan and the kingdom of darkness for mankind by living a sinless life in the flesh... By His suffering and death at Calvary... By His triumph over death, hell, and the grave... In His making an open show of Satan's defeat... And in His Resurrection. After He presented His blood to the Father, and the Father's acceptance of that blood, Jesus returned to earth, and said something to His disciples that applies to all believers thereafter.

> **Matt. 28:18** And Jesus came and spake unto them, saying, All power [exousia] is given unto me in heaven and in earth.
> **Matt. 28:19** Go ye therefore, and teach all nations, baptizing them in the name of the Father, and of the Son, and of the Holy Ghost:
> **Matt. 28:20** Teaching them to observe all things whatsoever I have commanded you: and, lo, I am with you alway, *even* unto the end of the world. Amen.

In His Great Commission, He said, *"All authority is given unto me in heaven and in earth, Go ye therefore..."*

Jesus delegated the authority on the earth to His body on the earth.

THE GREATER ONE WITHIN

Authority is as strong as the power behind it. The authority of the traffic policeman is as strong as the civic government behind him.

The power behind the Body of Christ is the greatest power in all Creation—the power of God. That's why the Word of God declares, *"Greater is He that is in you, than he that is in the world"* (1 John 4:4).

> **1 John 4:1** Beloved, believe not every spirit, but try the spirits whether they are of God: because many false prophets are gone out into the world.
>
> **1 John 4:2** Hereby know ye the Spirit of God: Every spirit that confesseth that Jesus Christ is come in the flesh is of God:
>
> **1 John 4:3** And every spirit that confesseth not that Jesus Christ is come in the flesh is not of God: and this is that *spirit* of antichrist, whereof ye have heard that it should come; and even now already is it in the world.
>
> **1 John 4:4 Ye are of God,** little children, **and have overcome them: because greater is he that is in you, than he that is in the world.**

Who are the "them" that verse 4 says we have overcome? They are the evil spirits written about in verses 1-3.

We have overcome them. Why? Because the Greater One lives in us!

We have authority over the kingdom of darkness.

We have a *ministry in the heavenlies* from which we can

rule and reign over the kingdom of darkness that aims to divide and conquer America, our homes, our lives, our freedom.

1. *How You Can Pray in the End of Days,* Dr. Billye Brim, Prayer Mountain in the Ozarks, P.O.Box 40, Branson, MO 65615.

2. *The Authority of the Believer,* John A. MacMillan, Prayer Mountain in the Ozarks, P.O.Box 40, Branson, MO 65615.

3. Ibid. p. xiii.

4. *The Companion Bible,* Kregal Publications, Grand Rapids, MI 49501, Appendix 172.

CHAPTER 19

OUR MINISTRY IN THE HEAVENLIES

C hristians have the authority to keep their areas free from shooting sprees at local schools, churches, malls or public events. Christians have the authority to keep their areas free from epidemics of suicide. Christians have the authority to keep Satan from having high carnival in their homes and families. Christians have the authority to keep the heavenlies clear over their places of habitation. Wherever demon forces are the culprits, we have the authority to keep them at bay.

The authority of the believer comes with the new birth.

But believers must know about it. And they must know how to operate in it. It is operated from a seat of authority at the right hand of the Father on high. A seat every believer can rule from, because they are seated there in Christ.

THE BOOK OF EPHESIANS

The principles of the authority of the believer are set forth in this New Covenant Letter to the body of Christ.

All the Bible is for the church, but not all the Bible is about the church. The part of the Bible that is particularly about the church is in the New Testament Epistles. The Epistles tell you who you are, what you are, and what you have, because you are "In Him."

Ephesians, even among all the Epistles, is particularly pertinent to us today. You should read the first two chapters right now.

A great man of God encouraged believers to pray the prayers in those chapters for themselves every day. They are Spirit-given and anointed prayers that we may pray for ourselves or for other believers. I have personalized those prayers and prayed them almost every day for many years. The "spirit of revelation" that has come to me, has come as a result.

THE FIRST PRAYER

Ephesians 1:17-2:1, 4-6
17 That the God of our Lord Jesus Christ, the Father of glory, may give unto you [unto me] the spirit of wisdom and revelation in the knowledge of him:
18 The eyes of your [my] understanding being enlightened; that ye [I] may know what is the hope of his calling, and what the riches of the glory of his inheritance in the saints,
19 And what *is* the exceeding greatness of his power to us-ward who believe, according to the working of his mighty power,
20 Which he wrought in Christ, when he raised him from the dead, and set *him* at his own right hand in the heavenly *places,*
21 Far above all principality, and power, and might, and dominion, and every name that is named, not only in this world, but also in that which is to come:
22 And hath put all *things* under his feet, and gave him *to be* the head over all *things* to the church,
23 Which is his body, the fulness of him that filleth all in all.
1 And you [I, or we] *hath he quickened,* who were dead in trespasses and sins;...

> 4 But God, who is rich in mercy, for his great love where-with he loved us,
> 5 Even when we were dead in sins, hath quickened us to-gether with Christ, (by grace ye are saved;)
> 6 And hath raised *us* up together, and made *us* sit together in heavenly *places* in Christ Jesus:

This prayer is that we may have revelation in Him of three particular things. They all have to do with glory, and the glorious church, but we won't go into that here.

1. The hope of His calling.
2. The riches of the glory of His inheritance in the saints.
3. The exceeding greatness of His power *(dunamis)* toward usward who believe.

It is only number 3 that we will go into here.

QUOTING FROM MACMILLAN'S BOOK
THE AUTHORITY OF THE BELIEVER[1]

MacMillan's book is so outstanding that for the rest of this chapter, I am quoting from it. I am not using the smaller type, because I want you to read it.

The Authority of the Believer, John A. MacMillan, portions of Pages 5-23
When the Lord Jesus, the Captain of our salvation, was raised from the dead, the act of resurrection was accomplished through "the exceeding greatness of His [God's] power *[dunamis],* to usward who believe, according to the working *[energeian]* of the strength *[kratous]* of His might *[ischuous]*."

In this working there was such a putting forth of the divine omnipotence that the Holy Spirit, through the apostle, requires four [Greek] words to bring out the thought...their combination signifies that behind the fact of the resurrection of the Lord Jesus there lay the mightiest working recorded in the Word of God.

Having been thus raised from among the dead, Christ Jesus was exalted by God to His own right hand in the heavenlies...

The resurrection had been opposed by the tremendous "powers of the air": "all principality, and power, and might, and dominion, and every name that is named, not only in this world [*aion,* age] but also in that which is to come" (Ephesians 1:21).

The evil forces of the "age to come" had been arrayed against the purpose of God. They had, however, been baffled and overthrown, and the risen Lord had been enthroned "far above" them, ruling with the authority of the Most High.

To Usward Who Believe

All the demonstration of the glory of God, shown in the manifestation of His omnipotence, pointed manward. The cross of Christ, with what it revealed... shows us a representative Man overcoming for mankind and preparing, through His own incumbence, a throne and *a heavenly ministry* for those who should overcome through Him...

Christ and His people were raised together... The reviving of Christ expresses also the reviving of His people. That is to say the very act of God which raised the Lord from among the dead, raised also His body. Head and body are naturally raised together: Christ, the Head; His body the Church [ek-klesia, the assembly of believers in Him].

...Ephesians lifts the believer with the ascended Christ to the heavenlies where he is made a partaker of Christ's throne...

The Location of Authority

[Through] the elevation of the Lord's people with their Head, they are made to sit with Christ "in the heavenlies." Christ's seat is at the right hand of God. His people, therefore occupy "with Him" the same august position. This honor is not to a chosen few, but is the portion of all those who share the resurrection of the Son of God. It is the birthright of every true believer, of every born again child of God...

The right hand of the throne of God is the center of power of the whole universe, and the exercising of the power of the throne was committed unto the ascended Lord...

The elevation of His people with Him to the heavenlies has no other meaning than that they are made sharers...of the authority which is His. They are made to sit with Him; that is, they share his throne. To share a throne means without question to partake of the authority which it represents.

Indeed, they have been thus elevated in the plan of God, for this very purpose, that they may even now exercise, to the extent of their spiritual apprehension, authority over the powers of the air and over the conditions which those powers have brought about on the earth and are still creating through their ceaseless manipulations of the minds and circumstances of mankind.

Rebel Holders of Authority

It is necessary to state here what is commonly understood by those who carefully study the Word, that the kingdoms of this world are under the control and leadership of satanic principalities. The great head of these is, in the Gospel of John, three times acknowledged as "prince of this world" by our Lord Himself. His asserted claim to the suzerainty of the world kingdoms, made in the presence of the Lord Jesus (Luke 4:6), was not denied by Christ.

Although a rebel against the Most High and now under judgment of dispossession (John 12:31), he is still at large, and as the masses of mankind are also rebels, he maintains over them an unquestioned, because unsuspected, rule, their eyes being blinded to his dominance (2 Corinthians 4:4)...

The Divine Purpose of the Ages

The "God of the whole earth" does not purpose to tolerate forever this rebellion against His righteousness. (See Isaiah 45:23.)

God...having redeemed a people and purified them, has introduced them potentially into the heavenlies...

This purpose, present and future, is very definitely stated in Ephesians 3:9-11 as the divine will that "now" (*nun*, the present time) unto the principalities and powers in the heavenly places might be made known through the church the manifold wisdom of God" (3:10). The church is to be God's instrument in declaring to these rebellious and now usurping powers, the divine purpose...

This is further declared to be "according to the eternal purpose of the ages which He purposed in Christ Jesus our Lord" (3:11).

...God through all the past ages, has had in view this wonderful plan of preparing in Christ Jesus a people, chosen, and called and faithful, whom He might place in these heavenly seats to rule through the ages to come.

Far Above

Christ sits far above all...

...He fills "all in all," but has chosen to do so through His Body...

"Hath put all things under His feet" (1:22).

The feet are members of the Body. How wonderful to think that the least and lowest members of the Body of the Lord, those who in a sense are the very soles of the feet, are far above all the mighty forces we have been considering, yet so it is. What need for the Church to awake to an appreciation of her mighty place of privilege. Exalted to rule over the spiritual powers of the air, how often she fails in her ministry of authority or grovels before them in fear.

Head over All

"Head over all things to the church which is His Body" (1:22).

We have little grasped the force of this marvelous truth... Let us reverse the words to bring out more clearly their deep significance: "Head to the church over all things." His being Head over all things is for the Church's sake, that the Church,

His Body, may be head over all things through Him. We need to sit reverently and long before these mighty truths, that their tremendous meaning may grasp our hearts. In this attitude, the Spirit of Truth can lift us into their comprehension, which the human mind alone will always fail to comprehend.

The Failure of the Church

...Why, then is there not more manifest progress? Because a head is wholly dependent upon its body for the carrying out of its plan...The Lord Jesus...is hindered in His mighty plans and working, because His Body has failed to appreciate the deep meaning of His exaltation and to respond to the gracious impulses which He is constantly sending for its quickening...

...God help us to realize this and to fulfill our ministry through the Word both to others and to the Lord.

---

1. *The Authority of the Believer,* John A. MacMillan, Prayer Mountain in the Ozarks, P.O.Box 40, Branson, MO 65615.

Chapter 20

How to Minister From The Heavenlies

Many times when someone describes to me how devils are having high carnival in their lives, I give them Mac-Millan's book, and I tell them, "Read this book. *And do page 27.*" So first of all, page 27 is quoted verbatim below. I took the liberty to italicize the part that is prayer.

Quote:

Do we believe that God "hath quickened us together with Christ and hath raised us up together, and made us sit to-gether in heavenly places in Christ Jesus" (Ephesians 2:5-6)? If we do, our reaction to it will be a fervent, *"Lord, I accept Thy gracious word. I believe that Thou hast thus wrought for me. In humble faith I do now take my seat in the heavenly plac-es in Christ Jesus at Thy right hand. Teach me how to fulfill this sacred ministry, how to exercise the authority which Thou hast entrusted to me. Train me day by day that I may attain to the full stature of the perfect man in Christ, so that in me, Thy purpose of the ages may be fulfilled. Amen."*

If we are walking in the Spirit, our normal life is in the heavenlies. To secure the consciousness of this, there must

be the daily acceptance of the fact. Let us morning by morning, as one of our first acts of worship, take our seat with
Christ (as suggested in the previous paragraph) and return
thanks to God for all that it implies. Let us often remind ourselves that we are seated far above all the powers of the air,
and that they are in subjection to us. As our faith learns to
use the Name and the Authority of Jesus, we shall find the
spiritual forces yielding obedience in ways that will surprise
us. As we continue to abide closely in Him, our prayers for
the advancement of the kingdom will become less and less
the uttering of petitions and will increasingly manifest the
exercise of a spiritual authority that...binds the forces of
darkness...[1]
Endquote.

How I Do It

It is the Lord's will that believers rule and reign over the
forces of darkness.

> **Rom. 5:17** For if by one man's offence death reigned by
> one; much more they which receive abundance of grace
> and of the gift of righteousness shall reign in life by one,
> Jesus Christ.) (KJV)

> **Rom. 5:17** For if because of one man's trespass (lapse,
> offense) death reigned through that one, much more sure-
> ly will those who receive [God's] overflowing grace (un-
> merited favor) and the free gift of righteousness [putting
> them into right standing with Himself] reign as kings in
> life through the one Man Jesus Christ (the Messiah, the
> Anointed One). (Amplified Bible)

Almost every morning, I rule and reign. I do my ministry in

the heavenlies. I do it from a seated position since I am seated with Him at the right hand of the Father. At home, I do this from my comfortable prayer chair.

First, I pray the prayer which begins in Ephesians Chapter One.

I start praying with verse 17, but I do not stop at the end of the chapter; I continue with Ephesians 2:1 and then skip to 2:4-6, or 7.

Here is an example of my prayer and how I rule and reign:
God of our Lord Jesus Christ, the Father of Glory,
Please give unto me the spirit of wisdom and revelation,
*   in the knowledge of Him:*
Let the eyes of my understanding be enlightened;
That I may know what is
*   The hope of His calling*
*   The riches of the Glory of Your inheritance in the*
*   saints.*
*   And the exceeding greatness of Your **dunamis** to*
*   us-ward who believe,*
*   According to your mighty power,*
*   which You wrought in the Messiah, The Anointed One,*
*   when you raised Him from the dead*
*   and set Him at your own right hand in the heavenlies.*
F-a-a-r A-b-o-v-e
*   all principality, and power, and might, and dominion,*
*   and every name that is named,*
*   not only in this age and world, but also in that which*
*   is to come.*
And You have put all under His feet,

And gave Him to be the Head over all to the eklesia (church),
   which is His Body,
   the fullness of Him that filleth all in all.
And me, have you quickened, when I was dead, slain by my
   trespasses and sins...
But God, who is rich in mercy,
For His great love wherewith He loved me,
Even when we were dead in sins,
   Hath quickened us together with Christ,
   (by grace we are saved)
   And hath raised us up together
   And made us sit together in the heavenlies in Christ Jesus.
When He quickened Him; He quickened me.
When He raised Him; He raised me.
When He seated Him; He seated me in Him.
Therefore in Him, I am seated far above all principality, power,
might and dominion, and every name that is named.
And in the Name of Jesus I will now rule and reign over the
powers of darkness, because the Lord told me to in Romans
5:17. For I have received abundance of grace and of the gift of
righteousness, therefore I now reign as a king in my life by one,
Jesus Christ.
Kingdom of darkness, listen to me. I hold the blood of Jesus
over all things pertaining to me and I forbid your having any-
thing to do with...

   From here, I follow my spirit. I start with family. Usually I
name them. Then I plead the blood over myself—spirit, soul,
and body. (See my book, *The Blood and The Glory*.)[2] I move
then to "the good works He has ordained that I should walk

in." I name them and their locations. And the people and places adjoined to me in these good works. I cover houses, properties, vehicles, etc.

I have authority over the powers of the air which operate through the sons of disobedience in my area, where I live, where I serve the Lord. I call it *habitational* authority. From time to time, as I am praying "first of all" for governmental leaders and I am in the spirit, the Lord grants me an anointing to exercise authority over the prince of the power of the air that would operate in Washington D.C., etc.

Believers who live in the greater Washington D.C. area can daily exercise their *habitational* authority over the demons who would operate there.

As to *habitational* authority, for instance, Branson, Missouri is one of the top tourist destinations in America. Terrorists would like to strike here. But those who regularly come to *Prayer Mountain in the Ozarks* for our Wednesday and Sunday corporate prayer services, know how to reign from their seats in Christ at the right hand of the Father. We know how to stop the strategies of the evil spirits who would work down through men to carry out demonic plots here.

Believers sitting in their seats of authority can keep evil plots from coming to fruition in their realms of authority. Believers exercising their ministry in the heavenlies can stop demonically driven riots and protests that would become violent. But it must be done on a daily basis.

Believers do not have authority over people or their wills. We have authority over demons. And we know that demons work down through men as it is written in the very portion of scripture that records the prayer we are praying.

> **Eph. 2:1** And you *hath he quickened,* who were dead in trespasses and sins;
> **Eph. 2:2** Wherein in time past ye walked according to the course of this world, **according to the prince of the power of the air, the spirit that now worketh in the children of disobedience:**
> **Eph. 2:3** Among whom also we all had our conversation in times past in the lusts of our flesh, fulfilling the desires of the flesh and of the mind; and were by nature the children of wrath, even as others.
> **Eph. 2:4** But God, who is rich in mercy, for his great love wherewith he loved us,
> **Eph. 2:5** Even when we were dead in sins, hath quickened us together with Christ, (by grace ye are saved;)
> Eph. 2:6 And hath raised *us* up together, and made *us* sit together in heavenly *places* in Christ Jesus:

A PLACE OF SAFETY

MacMillan points out that we occupy this place in faith, humility, boldness, and courage. He writes:

> But with this courage, there must be a continual and close abiding in God, a spirit that is alert to every urge and check from Him and a mind that is steeped in the word of God...

> *The Panoply of God*
> The only place of safety is the occupation of the seat itself. It is "far above" the enemy. If the believer abides steadfastly by faith in this location, he cannot be touched.
> Consequently the enemy puts forth all his "wiles" to draw him down in spirit, for once out of his seat, his authority is gone, and he is no longer dangerous,

and further, he is open to attack.

At this point is seen the meaning of the message of Ephesians chapter 6. To maintain his place against the wiles of the devil, the believer must be constantly arrayed in full armor.[3]

Wigglesworth said, "There is a place in God that Satan dare not come." This is the place, seated with Him at the right hand of the Father.

CHIP BRIM AND THE BRANSON TORNADO

On the 29th day of February, 2012, a tornado that was 400 yards wide and was on the ground for about 20 miles, tore through Branson, Missouri. It traveled east along Highway 76, the entertainment strip, damaging and destroying theaters, motels, and businesses. After wiping out much within its path, it headed straight toward Chip and Candace Brim's home.

Chip said that it sounded like a freight train as it stormed toward them at about 1:30 in the morning.

Down on the basement level of the house, which was also living quarters, Candace was pleading the blood. Chip was sitting in his seat in the heavenlies, doing exactly as described herein—reigning in his domain.

The house was shaking. The windows were heaving.

He said, "Mom, it wasn't easy, but I was doing it."

He told me how a phrase came out his mouth that he did not think of in his head.

He repeated it over and over, "Not one shingle. Not one shingle. Satan, you can't have one shingle."

When the storm died, they went outside. Just to the south of the house, a huge tree was uprooted. Across the way, and up a little rise, businesses were badly hit and didn't reopen for months. To the north, the house next door, and the houses all the way to the corner, were badly damaged. The roofs of many were gone. *Not one shingle* was gone from the Brim's roof. And everything else was intact.

Fox News came. In their television report, they compared the badly damaged house next door to the Brim house. Panning the camera to the Brim home, they used these exact words, "Not one shingle of this house is gone."

A week or so later, I was in the insurance office that we both use. I only needed to see a clerk, but the owner of the agency came out to see me. He said, "I went to Chip's to see what kind of damage he had. Not one shingle of his house was damaged." Again he used the exact words.

Chip posted it on YouTube that very day. At this point in time, you can watch it by searching: *Chip Brim, Branson tornado.*

ABOVE THE FRAY

In corporate prayer at *Prayer Mountain in the Ozarks,* the pray-ers here and those who join us by live streaming, make it a point to be cognizant of our position in prayer. No matter what we are praying about, we call to mind, and often speak from our lips, that we are praying from our God-given position at the Father's right hand.

Once, some years back, the Spirit of the Lord warned me that some trouble was coming. He didn't tell me what it was.

But He said to me, *"I want you to live above the fray."*

I recognized the trouble when it came. But I had my instructions. I had the peace of God from my view above the fray.

In the mid 1980s, I noticed a pattern in severe satanic attacks against my family. So I went to Kenneth E. Hagin. He told me, based on Isaiah 54:17, "As long as you are in this world, you can't keep weapons from being formed against you, but you can keep them from prospering."

So, I did just that. I used my authority and stopped them.

Sitting in one's seat every morning, is a way to do this. With authority and the shield of faith, we can "quench all the fiery darts of the wicked one" (Ephesians 6:16).

Always remember, when you are considering Ephesians 6 and its statement about wrestling, and the prayer armor, that Chapter 6 is a part of the same Epistle that begins with the amazing revelation of our being seated with and in Christ at the right hand of the Father. Consistently see yourself seated there.

> **Col. 3:1** If ye then be risen with Christ, seek those things which are above, **where Christ sitteth on the right hand of God.**
> **Col. 3:2** Set your affection on things above, not on things on the earth.
> **Col. 3:3** For ye are dead, and your life is hid with Christ in God.
> **Col. 3:4** When Christ, who is our life, shall appear, then shall ye also appear with him in glory.

I love this wonderful instruction from Colossians. Consider that while we are seeking those things which are above, it specifically emphasizes *"where Christ sitteth on the right hand of God,"* and remember that you are seated there in Him.

1. *Authority of the Believer,* John A. MacMillan, Prayer Mountain in the Ozarks, P. O. Box 40, Branson, MO 65615, pp 27, 28.

2. *The Blood and The Glory,* Dr. Billye Brim, Harrison House Publishers, Tulsa, OK.

3. *Authority of the Believer,* MacMillan, pp 28-31.

CHAPTER 21

DO WHAT THEY DID

As I wrote earlier, I did not cover the great revival that swept the country under the ministry of Charles G. Finney. Wesley Duewel writes, "The people who were led to Christ directly or indirectly by Finney through his personal campaigns, writings, encouragements, and prayer probably brought a million people or more into the kingdom of God."[1]

Prayer preceded and continued in every place there was a mighty outpouring of the Spirit during the Finney revival.

In central New York state, "Finney urged the people to pray to God earnestly and expectantly for 'the immediate outpouring of His Holy Spirit.'"

> "He told them that if they united in prayer, they would get God's answer quicker than a letter could come from Albany, the state's capital. Several men agreed to prove God in that way, and their prayer was answered just that quickly. Finney wrote, 'Indeed the town was full of prayer. Go where you would, you heard the voice of prayer. Pass along the streets, and if two or three Christians happened to be together they were praying. Wherever they met they prayed...'"[2]

An observer in New York City wrote, "Probably no man, since the days of Whitefield, ever stirred the minds of men in this city so widely and deeply, in their relations to practical and personal religion, as this great and good man. Preaching and praying were his only weapons. He surrounded himself with an atmosphere of prayer, and a body of devoted praying and working Christians male and female..."[3]

There was a man known as Father Nash who went ahead of Finney into the various cities and towns. This praying man prevailed in prayer. As did Finney himself.

If We Do What They Did

A skeptic had a large, flourishing high school in Rochester. A number of the students attended the Finney meetings and became deeply convicted of their need for Christ. One morning after the meetings had continued for two weeks, the principal found so many students weeping over their sins in the classrooms that he sent for Finney to come and instruct them. Finney came, and the principal and almost every student were converted. More than forty of the male students and a number of the female students in time became ministers or missionaries.

One of the girls in that school became the wife of Titus Coan. The Coans went to Hawaii as missionaries, and seven years later they were leaders in the mighty revival that came in full tide to Hawaii.[4]

I was in Hilo, Hawaii where the Coan's knew a mighty outpouring. And this is how it began.

Titus Coan said, "If we do what Finney did, then we can get what Finney got." They did it. And they got it.

God wants America to know another Great Awakening. If we do what they did in the prior Awakenings, then we will get what they got. An Awakening that will save America and bring her into the destiny for which she was designed by God.

I so remember the power of the Word that came forth in our Sunday afternoon prayer meeting June 29, 2008, as we were fervently praying about the upcoming elections:

One thing will save America.
And it is NOT the election.
It is an Awakening to God!
One thing will avail for Israel and the nations.
It is an Awakening to God!

Our instructions were, along with many others across America, I believe, to pray in an Awakening. We can. And we must!

---

1. *Revival Fire,* Wesley Duell, Zondervan, Grand Rapids, MI, p. 92.
2. Ibid. p. 101.
3. Ibid. p. 112.
4. Ibid. p. 107.

CHAPTER 22

FIRST OF ALL FOR LEADERS

On Mother's Day Sunday 2011, we received another assignment at *Prayer Mountain in the Ozarks* corporate prayer. I'd gone to bed the night before thinking of the power of a certain mother's prayer, Hannah, the mother of Samuel. At prayer the next day, we were made to know that Awakenings need leaders. And we were to pray them in.[1] (And when I say "we" it includes far more than just our assembly that day at *Prayer Mountain.*)

THE KING MESSIAH

Israel was in dire straits when Hannah prayed. Israel's leader at the time was the high priest, Eli. He was old and his sons, to whom the priesthood was to fall, were in gross sin. The Philistines were terrorizing Israel. Satan was surely behind it all, trying to bring down God's chosen nation.

But God! He was at work. He closed a woman's womb and gave her an *intense desire* for a son. So intense was her desire that she promised to give her son to the Lord. When she brought the child Samuel to Eli she gave a prophetic prayer of praise and thanksgiving that I've heard Jews say is one of the most highly regarded in the Bible (1 Samuel 2:1-10).

Hannah prayed in a son, Samuel. He became the leader Israel had to have at the time.

He was not, however, the only leader her prayer birthed. For in her prophetic prayer she said, *"...the barren hath born seven"* (I Samuel 2:5).

Yet when we count the natural children Hannah physically bore, there were only six. *"...three sons and two daughters. And the child Samuel..."* (I Samuel 2:21).

Who was the seventh? Or, actually, the First?

The answer is in verse 10 of her prophetic prayer, *"...the LORD shall judge the ends of the earth: and He shall give strength unto His King, and exalt the horn of His Anointed (Messiah)."*

This is the first mention of His Anointed One, the Messiah. It is the first mention of Him as The King Messiah. Hannah indeed bore seven. Her prayer birthed The King Messiah.

AWAKENINGS NEED LEADERS

That Mother's Day Sunday we received a new prayer assignment. The Lord made us to know that Awakenings need leaders. Spiritual leaders. And even governmental leaders. We knew we were to add to our prayers for an Awakening, prayers for its leaders.

The First Great Awakening knew George Washington. The Fourth Great Awakening knew Abraham Lincoln.

How important it must be if the Lord exhorted us to "First of All..."

1 Tim. 2:1 I exhort therefore, that, **first of all,** supplications, prayers, intercessions, *and* giving of thanks, be made for all men;

1 Tim. 2:2 For kings, and *for* all that are in authority; that we may lead a quiet and peaceable life in all godliness and honesty.

1 Tim. 2:3 For this *is* good and acceptable in the sight of God our Saviour;

1 Tim. 2:4 Who will have all men to be saved, and to come unto the knowledge of the truth.

Won't you commit to "first of all" in your daily prayers pray "for presidents, prime ministers, and for all who are in authority." According to the Word of the Lord it will be effective and God can get His will into the earth because someone on earth asked Him.

America can finish her God-given course. America can, will, and must reach her destiny. And that depends upon the prayers of God's people. That depends on you and me.

---

1. *Letters to Partners August 2008 to October 2011,* Dr. Billye Brim. Prayer Mountain in the Ozarks, P.O. Box 40, Branson, MO, 65615, pp. 97, 98.

BIBLIOGRAPHY

BOOKS

Baldwin, Alice M., *The New England Clergy and the American Revolution*, New York, NY: Frederick Ungar, 1958.

Bancroft, George, *History of the United States of America,* Vol. 4, D. Appleton & Co., New York, 1889.

Brim, Dr. Billye, *How You Can Pray in the End of Days*, Prayer Mountain in the Ozarks, P.O.Box 40, Branson, MO 65615.

Brim, Dr. Billye, *Letters to Partners in the Service of the Lord*, Prayer Mountain in the Ozarks, P.O.Box 40, Branson, MO 65615.

Brim, Dr. Billye, *The Blood and the Glory,* Harrison House Publishers, Tulsa, OK.

Chambers, Talbot W., *The New York City Noon Prayer Meeting, A Simple Prayer Meeting that Changed the World,* Published by Campus Renewal Ministries, 2009, 2421 San Antonio St., Suite B, Austin TX. Reprinted with permission from Global Harvest Ministries, Colorado Springs, CO.

Carnduff, M.Th., David, *Ireland's Lost Heritage*, IPCB Publications, printed by Antrim Printers Steeple Industrial Estate, Antrim, BT41 1 AB, 2003.

Dudley, Dorothy, *The Cambridge of 1776,* with the diary of Dorothy Dudley, 1876.

Duewel, Wesley L., *Revival Fire,* Zondervan, Grand Rapids, MI, 1995.

Edwards, Jonathan, *Jonathan Edwards on Revival,* Select Works of Jonathan Edwards, The Banner of Truth Trust, 3 Murrayfield Road, Edinburgh EH12 6EL, PO Box 621, Carlisle, PA 17013.

Franklin, Benjamin, *The Autobiography of Benjamin Franklin,* New York: Airmont, 1965.

Harland, Marion, *The Story of Mary Washington,* 1892.

Harrell Jr., David Edwin, Edwin S. Gaustad, John B. Boles, Sally Foreman Griffith, *Unto a Good Land: A History of the American People,* ISBN-13: 978-0802837189.

Hyatt, Eddie L., *2000 Years of Charismatic Christianity*, Charisma House, Lake Mary, FL.

Hyatt, Eddie L., *The Faith & Vision of Benjamin Franklin,* Hyatt Press, PO Box 3877, Grapevine, TX.

Hyatt, Eddie L., *Pilgrims and Patriots,* Hyatt Press, PO Box 3877, Grapevine, TX.

Johnson, William J., *George Washington, The Christian,* The Abingdon Press, NY, Cincinnati, Copyright 1919.

Kidd, Thomas S., *George Whitefield: America's Spiritual Founding Father,* New Haven: Yale University Press, 2014.

MacMillan, John A., *The Authority of the Believer*, Prayer Mountain in the Ozarks, P.O.Box 40, Branson, MO 65615.

Marshall, Peter and Manuel, David, *THE LIGHT AND THE GLORY, God's Plan for America 1492-1793,* Revised and Expanded Edition, Revell division of Baker Publishing Group, Grand Rapids, MI.

Novak, Michael, *On Two Wings: Humble Faith and Common Sense at the American Founding,* San Francisco: Encounter, 2002.

Peckham, Colin & Mary, *SOUNDS FROM HEAVEN, The Revival on the Isle of Lewis, 1949-1952,* Christian Focus Publications, Geanies House, Fearn, Ross-shire, IV20 ITW, Scotland.

Pollock, John C., *GEORGE WHITEFIELD, The Evangelist,* Christian Focus Publications, Ltd, Geanies House, Fearn, Ross-shire, IV20 1TW, Great Britain.

Rossiter, Clinton, *Seedtime of the Republic,* New York: Harcourt, Brace and Co., 1953.

Sparks, Jared, *The Writings of George Washington,* 12 Vols., 1837.

Rosell, Garth M. and Richard A.G. Dupuis, ed.,*The Memoirs of Charles G. Finney,* Zondervan, Grand Rapids, MI, 1989.

Stewart, Linda, *The Other Cape,* American Heritage (at: www.americanheritage.com/articles/magazine/ah/2001/2/2001_2_50).

Waters, Thomas Franklin & Mrs. Eunice Whitney Farley Felten, *Top Ipswich Patriots,* Lord Family Album, 1927 (at: www.bw-lord.com/Ipswich/Waters/TwoPatriots/JohnWise).

George Whitefield's Journals, The Banner of Truth Trust, 3 Murrayfield Road, Edinburgh EH 12 6EL, P. O. Box 621 Carlisle, PA.

Wise, John, *A Vindication of the Government of New England Churches: and the Churches' Quarrel Espoused,* Boston: Congregational Board of Publication, 1860.

ARTICLES

Rev. Jonas Clark and the Battle of Lexington April, 1775. Article excerpted from *America's Providential History* by Mark Beliles and Stephen McDowell. Order from the *Providence Foundation Store.*

Evangelism in Patrick Henry's "Liberty or Death" Speech, Thomas Kidd, found online at: WE'RE HISTORY.

The Gilder Lehrman Institute of American History, www.gilder-lehrman.org

BIBLES

Amplified
King James Version

The Companion Bible, with Notes and Appendixes by E. W. Bullinger, Kregal Publications, Grand Rapids, MI.

The Founders' Bible, Signature Historian David Barton, Shiloh Road Publishers, 4680 Calle Norte, Newbury Park, CA 91320. ISBN 978-1-61871-001-7.

About the Author

Billye Brim's Christian heritage is rich. She sensed the call of God in early childhood. However, it was only after an encounter with the Holy Spirit in 1967, that she as a young wife and mother of four began to follow Him to walk out her call. For almost ten years she served as Editor of Publications for Kenneth E. Hagin Ministries where she also taught at Rhema Bible Training Center.

Immediately after ordination in 1980 she traveled to Soviet Russia in what proved to be ongoing ministry there. Since then she has literally ministered around the world several times over.

Kent and Billye Brim with Lee and Jan Morgans founded a local church in Collinsville, Oklahoma. A Glorious Church Fellowship is the foundation of Billye Brim Ministries and Prayer Mountain in the Ozarks in Branson, Missouri, and the soon-to-be-built Migdal Arbel Prayer and Study Center in Israel.

When Kent passed away in 1986, Billye was led to "study Hebrew in the Land." Studying at Ulpan Akiva in Israel led to the unique Seminar Tours she has guided in the Land from 1986 to now. It also provided a pattern for the Prayer and

Study Center in Israel.

"Helping Pray-ers" is a God-given directive in her life. One place this happens is at Prayer Mountain in the Ozarks near Branson, Missouri. On 300 plus acres, log cabins provide places for individual prayer, or small prayer groups. Corporate prayer meetings are held twice a week in the chapel.

On Wednesdays at 12 Noon CST, the meeting is streamed live. Pray-ers, who have named themselves World-Wide Pray-ers (WWPs), join in united prayer via thousands of computers in more than 60 nations. This prayer is focused primarily on an Awakening to God. For in a corporate prayer meeting in June 2008, Billye Brim and the pray-ers were impressed with these words: *One thing will save America...an Awakening to God. One thing will avail for Israel and the nations, An Awakening to God.*

She also hosts an *Autumn Assembly of Prayer* in Branson each fall, where several thousand pray-ers from around the world gather.

First Corinthians 10:32 is foundational in Billye Brim's ministry. The "good works that He has ordained that she should walk in" involve activity among the Jews, the Nations, and the Church—all to the Glory of God.